Imperfectly Sane

Stacy Lee Hoch

ISBN: 1546644679
ISBN 13: 9781546644675

An Introduction

THIS IS NOT the book I needed to write. It's a story that wrote me, more than I wrote it. This is the book I needed to *read*.

I believe that when we collectively become fully embodied as a group of people, we'll all be entrepreneurs sharing our God-given gifts with other God-given gift givers.

The balance that's possible between us, when we who *know* ourselves, who stands in our value and takes authority over our space, but never take away from others, is something I want to be a part of creating on this dimension *(dead or alive)*.

There are gifts in the gifts I've been given that are given you, woven through these words that've threaded their way right to your hands. A mark of our one-ness. Though resistance may be at the forefront of your self-actualization, I don't believe anyone who reads this book in its entirety isn't unconsciously dedicated to their healing in the only kind of healing that actually heals it *all*.

Vulnerable, naked, but newly unafraid to be seen, releasing this has by far been the greatest death my ego has faced yet. A good teacher trusts life's rhythms that let them know when it's their time to preach and when it's their time to practice, and knows that preach and practice at times, come together like rain and sun, meeting each other in a colorful dance in the sky. On a practical note, this preach is a deepening dedication to my decades of soul exercising practices and is a mark of what it really means to let go.

It will likely be ostracizing, but where we belong, is on the platform of our *own truth*. Here, I will stand. No longer will my stance be contingent upon concerns of being rejected or accepted. Simply, because life is a metaphor for the lenses we see through and living based on contingencies of others, *not being living at all*, is a large part of the moral of this story.

My disclaimer is simple: I saw life, the way I saw it, and potentially, I'm perfectly insane.

Maybe some of it, none of it, or all of it, happened exactly as I saw it. But maybe, my sight required glasses *(in a sixth sense way if you know what I mean)*. Whether or not this is true, it is my story. But a story is a made up reality after all whether we're reading it, or we're writing it. Even when our stories are true, truth (stories portray) is subject to a specific angle, not a panorama.

If someone would've handed me this book when I was eighteen, though I probably wouldn't have read it because I was a piss ant at the time, if I *had*, I'd have felt heard, *felt*, and gifted the vibration of home for the first time in my cognitive life.

The funny thing is, this book *was* handed to me at eighteen. By God, it actually was I just didn't see it until right this very second! If you'd have told me this story was the one I'd be reading, written by my own hands, when I was eighteen, I would've probably cried and begged you to just take me to the part where the story gets good. I'd have begged you to show me, to save me, but I'd also have thanked you for believing that the little engine that is me, *could*. Here now, I know, had I skipped to the *good* part, I wouldn't have found a way to live in the middle of my story. The middle of our story is the flesh, the beginning bones, and the ending, skin. Where skin ends, the world only begins. The middle though, the flesh, is where we allow ourselves to be nourished, or be eaten. Without the flesh, there would be no skin, and without the skeleton, there would be no flesh. The middle is what moves us. To be moved from the inside out, is to be alive.

The road to get to Imperfectly Sane, which is what I believe this is, has a message for us all. You know those things in life that you didn't know you needed until you got it? This might be one of them. If you're into considering some glasses for your soul of sorts, read on. If you're brave enough to actually put them on, write on!

Searching To Hide While Wanting To Be Found.

"Three things cannot be long hidden: the sun, the moon, and the truth."

—Buddha

YOU KNOW WHEN you're super hungry and your body starts in with anxiety-like symptoms of the shakes? When you finally get food, distractedly high strung, you devour it without even tasting it.

Once your meal ends, reprieved, your exhale is one of overindulgent fullness. Somewhat sloth like, somewhat surrendered to whatever happens next because no matter what it is, *at least* you ate.

That last part is what it's like to be with Chris.

I've been hungry for intimacy, on the prowl with nervous insecurities that even on a good night's sleep, I couldn't run away from with the highest tech running shoes.

I've been in quite loving relationships that though I was eating from, I still had an insatiable desire to hold onto the anxiety of the hunger that I had previous to it.

I was in it, but never let myself relax enough to actually taste it. I've spent enough time in deprivation chambers to know that I'm wired for the chase in nothingness which is a huge metaphor for fears game.

When we close our eyes really tight, we'll see black. We can make up a shit ton of dramas in the dark. A story may be true, but when we're the main character of our lives, we get to determine the truth we give the story.

If we look a little closer with our eyes closed, what we'll *really* see is a bunch of white dots that together make up a solar system of collective light. Light leaves little room to make up stories. It expands itself into the void by giving birth to new life, not digesting someone else's shit. We're all lone stars making our way in the dark, to a galaxy like our self that we might call God. Without each star, the creator would not be whole.

And then, there was him. It wasn't until I met him that I understood the profundity of seeing my light while I was looking for a galaxy in the dark. He taught me it'd be *my* light leading my way and that angels are warriors but if anyone was holding a candle on my path, it'd be *my* sunshine they were leading me toward.

There he was. The feeling *after* the meal.

The moment I saw him, I knew.

Not some love at first sight kind of fairy tale, but an honest to God, curious knowing that if it had to be expressed in a face, it would look like a squinty eye, poking fun in its gaze, saying, "I know something you don't know and it's us. Come find me out bitch."

Experiences that, in other relationships, would have triggered my uncertainty, and my self-sabotage tendencies, weren't there. Other women, other men, none of them phased what I knew since the moment I saw him. Time was of no threat to my certainty, nor the circumstances in the space between us.

I was the rain and he was the sunlight and I knew when we touched the same soil, whatever we grew together would have a life of its own. I let it grow as it wished, not as I wanted, excited to be around to watch it bloom.

My mother placed bets with the world that I'd never get married because I'm not the marrying type. I'd never find a partner who'd satisfy my desires for freedom or that I wouldn't kill for standing in my way of it *according to her.*

I moved through life anxious and hungry, gobbling up every meal on my table, only to be left anxious about the next, until I walked into the restaurant of *him.*

His atmosphere was just light enough that I could see, and dark enough that I didn't have to if I wasn't up for peering into my shadows.

His food was portioned with a healthy mix of goods and when I walked in, I knew if I ate there, I wouldn't be leaving lethargic from overindulgence of food that was no good for me. I'd be energized from the exact amount I needed and I wasn't sure I was ready to give up my gluttonous ways just yet, but I knew I wanted to. All my years of searching for who I'd be if I were found, would be over.

He cooked slowly, which riddled the impatience of my immediate gratification satiation tendencies. His calm, which is a very different kind from my own, taught me the value of slow cooking to release nutrients rather than killing them in a microwave.

Eventually, his unwavering patience and presence allowed me to relax enough to feel *full* after the meal.

The kind that it doesn't matter what happens next because you've already eaten. Stopping for fuel won't be necessary.

It wasn't my freedom I was searching for in my hot and cold attempts at being intimate with another human being.

Maybe all I was searching for was security after all.

Security has spoon fed me the highest sense of freedom I've ever known.

I didn't settle in with the best meal, or most rare, or the owner of the restaurant, but the chef who taught me how to cook. We'll never settle *down*, but always *in*.

Contrary to my previous belief, relationships aren't entrapment, they're a unified choice to explore our freedom, *together*. They're a culture of faith or a culture of fear and anything between is purgatory. Hanging out in the space between faith and fear, one foot in, one foot out, will never show us who we are when we step two feet into our own love story. We can't call our story our own unless we *own* it.

Being with him feels like the breath of surrender after I've eaten a meal I couldn't wait to eat, so I could move onto my to-do list. This book is a sigh of that surrender.

I know that I've found what some people never get to know and I do not take it for granted for one second.

Previously, I would've misjudged love as imprisonment, but true security is not a prison guard, it is the cell key. It frees us to begin to live the rest of our lives.

Securely tucked into love as a verb, is where true freedom lives.

I have found my home, but it is not in him.

Home *finds me* in the gratitude for the rhythm of his beat while I quietly focus, skin to skin, on his heart, listening like underwater sounds in a warm bath.

I have found home, in my *own* pulse.

In strength he came, handed me the mic, and gave me permission to speak even when my voice quivered and inducing vomit seemed like an easier medium to let him know where my heart stood.

Pulse baby, pulse. Listen.

He was the first person I trusted enough to listen to, so I did. Like the mirrors in our house that are covered in expo marker affirmations of grace, he held a reflection to my face that wasn't always pretty, was sometimes gorgeous beyond measure, was never, ever shaming, but was always, brutally honest.

It wasn't until security handed me the cell key to my own prison that I wrote the greatest love story I've ever written.

But love, isn't what my story is about. Or at least, that's not what I thought, while I spent the first twenty three years of my life writing it. My story, she bled.

Story She Bled.

"They may torture my body, break my bones, even kill me. Then they will have my dead body, not my obedience."

—*Ghandi*

I WAS TWENTY three the first time I wrote my life story. I locked myself in a bathroom, collected all of the things that could possibly harm my two toddler children and turned the shower on so I couldn't hear them. For two days, I locked myself in a bathroom to pour my heart out onto paper. It needed to have a life outside of myself. I needed to displace outwardly how insane it all was. My life had for the first time, gotten quiet enough for me to hear myself think and it led me down a river of rocks that each shifted when I walked on them. I couldn't see any way to solid ground. I was negligent for those two, twenty four hour days, but I had to write. Writing was the first bitch in a long time that seduced my fancy and I needed to spend time with her.

I didn't trust her much. Seduction had always been dangerous in my book. I didn't trust her intents or meaningless grandiose self-proclaiming purposes. I didn't trust that she wasn't my ego wanting to take revenge on the world that bruised it so terribly by gaining some notoriety for her knack for resilience via escapism. I didn't know if she was my guardian angel passing through all of the spaces between where my letters sat on a page, breathing me some new life that would leave me defenseless to this world I had worked so hard to defend my innocence against. Still, I let her come because I had just read a book that defended the integrity of people who cut themselves to feel better and I decided my days of scratching myself bloody were over. But honestly, I needed to bleed.

And my life story, she bled.

I could never finish my story. I refused to edit it because I had this blunt realization that this story, isn't over. There was more to come of the story I had written. So, I let it sit for a decade.

I first shared my story at a yoga retreat when I was twenty six. I told a woman who listened to me, that I had written about it. She looked appalled and said, "You wrote a book about your life? I wouldn't want to read it. Your life sounded horrible." Clearly, she liked me. We were eating lunch together, by choice. She was candid.

She was obviously missing the fact that sitting in front of her, were the "riches" in the old cliché "rags to riches" story I had purged onto paper and was sharing with her.

Her proclamation sat as a veil between my truth and everything that I felt like the world would let me say for almost a decade.

I didn't write. I changed.

Her allegiance to what she wanted to invite into her mind and heart by rejecting my story, challenged me. She was older, a mom, clearly seasoned in the life thing. Up until her, I sincerely thought that happy people didn't know shit about life. I thought they had never experienced one ounce of human sorrow and I could give two shits less to be interested in their stupidity. Plus, they bored me. It had honestly never occurred to me that despite circumstances, some happy people weren't stupid. That they did in fact feel the effects of the human experience, and were smart enough to have found their lives worth creating for.

Ironically, years later, I ran into that same woman at the same yoga center. We cheered as giddy, rabbit-like girls, hopping toward each other when we saw one another. The first thing coherent out of her mouth was, "Giiiirrrrrlll, I'm following you! And I LOVE what you're life is about and I just love your writing! You are really inspiring a lot of people! And, here you are!"

I giggled as I told her the story of when she had blatantly told me she'd never be interested in reading about my life. She didn't remember that conversation at all. But, I did.

My life story purge in the bathroom those two days went a bit like this:

My mother was a cunt. She was not the motherly type at all. She'll admit this. She tried to drown me when I was three for not wanting to take a bath. My dad told me she used to clap her hands and say "Yay!" at me when I was an infant, just for doing nothing if it's any consolation to how much I'll be leaving out in the brevity of my life story, up until age twenty three. My mother told me about once a year that the only reason she didn't abort me is because she wanted to see what I would look like.

"A child is a representation of the parent," according to her. She made all of my clothes and dressed me up as her doll while corroding any ounce of self-respect I may have gained from a mother that loved me in light, rather than vanity. Shame, she hoped to be her tool. I had faith it was her weapon.

She was physically, mentally, and emotionally abusive. The thing my father reports most about my mom's physicality is that I would beg, in tears, "What did I do? What did I do?" when she hit me for something I clearly didn't understand I had done. There was a rational response. She was not a teacher. She was a bully.

She never gave hugs or touch at all that didn't hurt. Two of my babysitters (separately) went to jail for child abuse or got shut down by the state multiple times (which my mother knew. She sent me there because it was "cheap").

My mother's father was an abuser, so she frequently reminded me of how "lucky" I was that I got her as a parent and not him. He was also an adulterer. Her mom was weakened to the notion of her victimhood and never thought otherwise, not even on her dying day. My mother's father beat my grandmother bloody, often hospitalizing her. He kicked all five kids and his wife out in blizzards with no transportation to get to nowhere, in the middle of the night. My grandmother stayed with him. She stayed with him after he had a baby with her brother's wife. She stayed with him after my aunt (her own daughter) came out and demanded people speak the truth about the sexual misconduct rampant in her childhood at the hands of my grandfather. My mother scoffed once, "Whatever happened to her, happened to all of us. She just needs to get over it," knowing her sister was eating away at herself in a psychiatric unit because the whole family either denied its reality by shutting her out or being quiet about it, implying to her that she shouldn't stir trouble.

My mother left me with her parents on their farm every summer. When my dad kicked my mom and I out when I was seven for his own adulterous romp, my mom and I lived at my grandparents. She was rushing me to get dressed, aggressively putting my shirt on as she pushed my little body side to side, with her fists hurrying the process. I asked her to stop which provoked her even more, until I screamed, "Rape!" My mother punched me in my right jaw and scolded with a clenched fist (and jaw) "Don't you ever say that word in this house! Ever! Do you understand me?! EVER!" I didn't cry that time. I didn't cry a lot of the times she hit me uncontrollably. That was my only sense of control. I didn't want to satisfy her with my tears.

I didn't cry that time but I did immediately know why she was saying I could never say that word in that house. Sex and anything associated with it was dirty, naughty, and filthy. My vagina was disgusting. Her legs were too fat, her tits too small, her stomach too round. Until I got to an age where *my* body began to take shape and every projection she placed on her own body, she licked all over mine with a demeaning tongue. The body was disgusting. Sex and the body: disgusting, shameful, evil, worthless, but *somehow*, necessary aspects of life.

She made me sleep with her until I was eleven. I begged her to let me sleep on my own and she would equally beg me to sleep with her, guilting me into it. Basically everything I did, I did for my mother.

She wanted a daughter who was a pianist, a dancer, a barbie doll. Well, not really. I'm pretty confident that my mother had no fucking clue what she wanted out of a daughter. Actually, my entrance into the world all together was a disappointment. They had told her I was a boy her entire pregnancy. She had always wanted a boy. More importantly for the times, I suppose, she had wanted to be the grand prize winner of my father by giving him a biological son after four daughters with another woman.

She put me in every activity imaginable for a lower middle class Pennsylvanian girl to explore her senses with, while also corrupting every interaction I had with it. She was the mother who encouraged piano playing. I'd play the piano and she'd scream that I wasn't doing it right.

So, I stopped practicing around her. She'd scream at me to practice. Then when I did practice, and sucked, she'd punch me in the face, rip me out to the car by my hair and scream the entire way in the car that I was telling my piano teacher that *very* night, within the hour that I was quitting forever and why? Because I didn't practice.

Then we'd get to piano lessons and she'd say, "Are you really gonna quit? I didn't raise a quitter! You better start practicing more."

Um, I knew what all of this meant. Which was, nothing. The consequence to everything was that there is a consequence *for* everything and that consequence will accomplish absolutely nothing.

As a pretty clear metaphor, her holding my head under water when I was three, about sums it up. She was the hand that held my hair and pushed my face underwater, and she was the hand that pulled my nose out at the last second so I could catch one more breath before her hand shoved me down again. When she pulled my face back up, she'd make me look at her hard, and thank her for letting me breathe.

On nights my father was home from work, she'd demand I sleep in my own bed, which was scary because there were ghosts in my parents' house. Usually though, she made me sleep with her. I overheard her making fun of me to one of *my* friends, laughing, repulsively "She's ten and she still sleeps with her mother."

Her commentary frequently included insults like, "No wonder you have no friends."

"No one is going to like you."

"What kind of a kid does, XYZ? I'll tell you what kind. A dumb shit."

I was inherently a very shy, sensitive and quiet kid. I was always an observer. I literally, never did know, what exactly I was doing wrong.

Gleefully, I sat on my living room floor playing with my new puppy when I was five. My mother and my cousin and my cousin's boyfriend stared me down, sitting on couches surrounding me. I was silently content, loving my dog. They stared disgusted, talking of what a spoiled brat I was, how ungrateful I was, how annoying I was. Nothing was worse than to hear myself being referred to as "annoying".

When I was five, my mother must have been going through some shit, or my memory receptors just opened for me because there is not a lot that I remember, but I do remember being five and my mother kicking me out. In front of my aunt and uncle, she told me I was going to a Boarding School that night and I needed to pack my clothes. I carried two bags up to my dark room and sobbed as I picked out my favorite clothes from my drawer and softly and longingly put them into brown paper grocery bags. I wept for the clothes I was being forced to leave behind. I told them all I loved them and I'd come save them when I could.

I did the same thing for my stuffed animals, and basically any object that let me love it without slapping me for my devotion to it. I promised everything I'd save it because I knew what it was like not to be saved and I wanted everything to know I not only saw it, but I'd take care of it at no cost. I'd just love it because it was lovable.

That night, my mother didn't kick me out. I sobbed down the stairs, turned the corner with my bags in hand. They all laughed at me, told me to go unpack and that I didn't have to go away that night, but maybe the next day. The next day, I didn't have to go.

When I was five, she did actually kick me out in the dark though.

My parents' house has a screen door and a very small walkway that can fit about three squished people into it before the interior wooden door. There I sat, in the dark, begging, sobbing, and pleading to be let in. No answer. When I had quieted to a smooth cry once again, that hand that pushed me out the door, opened it in its shiny savior armor and I was set free of the bondage of suffocation into a new breath that I should be thanking her for.

I did the same thing to my cousin once. He was young, in diapers young, at our house which was terribly unfamiliar to him. I was just big enough to carry him to the other side of the yard. I put him down and I ran away, hiding behind something I could still see him through. I waited to see his reaction up until I saw him pucker his lip, looking for anyone in sight. When he started to cry, I ran to save him. Then, I took him to another spot in the yard and repeated the same thing again. I practiced the art of living out my own desire for a savior by creating situations in which I was able to become one, which I'm sure is exactly what my mother was doing with me.

The cornerstone of my existence was confusion.

My dad, who I'll tell you about in a minute, looked at me one day as my mother was hitting me and with a twinkle in his eye said, "Who's bigger Stac? You or her?" I don't know what he meant by this, but his question felt like the key to my power. I had an overwhelming idea that one, he was giving me permission to unleash on my mother, and two, that I didn't have to take it after all. That I could indeed, look at myself with honor and not have to placate my mother's tendencies for catharsis, using me as her punching bag.

She's grabbed my firsts and screamed, "Punch me in my face" as she punched herself with my fists. I resisted making any movement with my body. She's attacked me and then held my arms down as she sat on top of me, begging me to tell her I love her.

Her biggest tool second to shame was also, like shame, a weapon. Gifts.

She'd go overboard on her limits of what she constituted as acceptable abuse and then she'd leave a nice material gift on my bed. Sometimes, she'd even apologize on bent knees right after her "blind rages," which is what she called them. But pretty consistently, her apology was silently met with a material possession. In this way, every gift I ever received came at a cost. I bought it first with her fists and then she delivered. Always, I heard very soon after the gift I had received, that she couldn't pay the mortgage that month because I was a spoiled brat. Always, I associated my survival as requiring suffering before it was met.

She also gave me peanut butter and jelly sandwiches rather than making me eat my meals if I didn't like them. She baked. Always. Food was our focus. We woke up talking about breakfast, lunch, and dinner. We went to bed talking about how shitty we felt from eating too much that day. Then she would slyly, point at my belly rolls and say, "You really do need to stop eating so much. Look at yourself. You think anyone's ever going to want you?"

Once I got so skinny that she said, "Start eating something. You have no tits anymore. That's gross." She even has a number for what *my* ideal weight is supposed to be, but when I'm at it, she comes up with something else I need to pursue perfecting in the body image category. This left me never good enough and always confused.

She volunteered sometimes. She looked like Betty Crocker to the world, but was a bare bones skeleton of drudgery to anyone who truly knew her. Basically, I was the only one who truly knew her.

I saw her cry tears, maybe eight times, ever. I saw her cry through her rage, blind or conscious, pretty daily with her actions.

She told me I was crazy and I believed her. She put me in counseling when I was very young, which even then, felt like a bad case of emotional Munchausen syndrome by proxy. She put me on antibiotics for sickness about once a month which was the spirit of the times.

I was perpetually sick. Like, always sick. She read me books at night on most nights, but told me I was lazy for not doing it myself.

My father is somewhat a mystery to me, though I know he fills in every gap of my story that I never really had to look at. My mother demanded focus. Focus on myself, focus on her. The only thing I ever remember my mother saying to me about my father besides, "Go ask your father…" was when he kicked us out and we lived at my grandparents. She told me my father only came to see me because she made him, but that he really didn't want to.

I wrote of a vivid memory in which I played with the rocks in our driveway while my father lifted weights in the garage. I believed he was the strongest man on earth and he would protect me from everything. Anything, including my mother.

He did once. I took a bath with my mother and wanted to be like her to gain some sort of acceptance. As she did, I picked up a razor. Not knowing my limits, I dug it into my leg and pulled up from my mid-calf to my knee. A bloody mess ensued. I screamed in internal chaos. My father ran into the bathroom and whisked me out of the tub. Their exchange was simple and short-lived. "Why the hell did you let her do that? She's a three year old girl! She doesn't know better!" My mother's response, with a nervous laugh at my father's redirection was, "If she wants to be stupid enough to play with razors, she's going to be stupid enough to cut herself with them." She finished up her bath and my savior father carried me away into a safe, dark, night.

He threatened her often. I remember him repeatedly saying, "If you leave black and blue marks on her, I'm going to kill you." Purple and yellow marks apparently didn't count, because I definitely had them.

He was gone. My vision for him was of a knight in shining armor coming to save me from the world he had brought me into. But really, he wasn't around to know the world I lived in.

My father defined himself by his time spent in Vietnam as a Staff Sargent in the marines. Before that, his life consisted of being shipped off from his home into living rooms of people who were willing to have him. His mother loved babies, but wasn't really interested in children. The youngest of six kids from two much-older-for-the-times parents, who had little intimate connection to him or anyone. His parents were hoarders and antique-junkies who volunteered to help the "needy" but never noticed the *needs* right under their nose.

When he left for Vietnam, his mother saw him off by saying only one thing. "Well, I hope to see you again." And she was serious. I mean, that's exactly, and *only,* what she meant. Naturally, his men became his family. He vowed to bring every man home, dead or alive, never expecting that he himself, would make it home again. He didn't care either. There was nothing for him in the life he left. The only life left for him was that of a war. A real one. Not the war against himself, or the cops and robbers and Army games he played in his childhood, but a war of physical combat, life for life, that no kid, just out of high school could comprehend before their immersion.

He was indoctrinated to listen. Much like me, he got his ass kicked for making mistakes he didn't know he was making and saying things that weren't the right answer to questions he was asked. What he was exactly listening to and for what reason, I'm sure he still doesn't know. As anyone in Vietnam who made it back home may have, he got spit on, shit on, and ridiculed for his part in a war he once believed would bring peace. He knows he fought for absolutely nothing. In that nothing though, as the old saying goes, "you can take the guy out of the war, but you can't take the war out of the guy," *nothing* changed *everything* for him.

Obviously, anyone who is willing to go to war anyway, is someone who is already at war with themselves. I've heard stories of my father's fights. Bar fights. One when he beat a guy senseless, pulled him over the bar and held his face under the tap flipping the lever to drench the guy in booze as his final statement. A drive by fight when he jumped on someone's windshield and beat a dude who was sleeping with his ex-wife as he drove down my father's street. You know, just, my-dad's-kind-of fights.

Underneath it all, he's a quiet, philosophical, lost, hopeful romantic, toughening himself up to protect his own from this cruel world he perceives we live in.

He came home from war, got his high school sweetheart knocked up and lived in a different kind of war zone through parties, sex, and raising five kids. (His ex-wife had two, they had three while they were married, one of which eventually both agreed upon, was *not* my father's biological child when the boy was four). Supposedly, my father missed my sister's delivery because he was sleeping with his eighteen year old neighbor when his wife went into labor. I only share this to say that he is a man who is desperate for anything real about intimacy, while also being deeply confused by it, but will do anything to have a taste no matter the cost.

My parents met after his divorce. My father didn't at first admit to having any kids. Later, he told my mom he had two (because they are his biological children according to his ex-wife, though growing up, he frequently disclosed to me that I was his only biological child as far as he was concerned).

My mom was a baker, sewer, gardener, worker bee, who valued materials as her way of giving the world the finger just to show it she was good enough too. My father was a thrill ride. Handsome, lost somewhere inside his armor. You know, the kind young girls secretly want to save from themselves, just to conquer the mask.

Five years later, when my mother had surgery to remove a dislodged IUD (birth control), they conceived me within the eight day window of her surgery and her new IUD's scheduled placement. They didn't want me. My father's first words when he was told I was a girl in the waiting room of the hospital were, "You've got to be kidding me. Put it back." He was referring to putting me back into my mother's womb.

We became a mixed family of seven, but a confused unit of three, trying to make our way in the world.

As far as I could see, where consciousness became a disservice is that we're the only animals on the planet who will raise our offspring just to torture them. Other species accept you as theirs, or they don't. There isn't ambiguity about whether someone does or doesn't belong. They make it very clear. You're in or you're out. They care for their young that can keep up. Or, they don't. But they will not invite an offspring into their pack for their own sadistic pleasures. They will either cut them out or care for them. Period.

Human consciousness fails here while also maintaining some kind of moral order in another right. People raise their children for unnatural reasons: pride, social acceptance, to care for the family farm, for their own emotional needs to be met. If you're lucky, people will raise you as if raising you is natural to them. It probably makes it feel like they love you and you're pretty certain that you can trust you belong to them. Ambiguity makes us question where we belong. Knowing where I belong has always been one of the only situations in life I want to be completely black or white about after years of living in the grey feeling like I was being held captive to it, only for torture. My presence was torturous to the people I loved. In turn, they tortured me, or so I thought. I never could tell if I was fully in or fully out of belonging with them.

Kids are impressionable and I was one. I believed everything they told me. My dad carried me into the ocean on his shoulders once and went in too deep for my fearful liking. I begged him to stop. He screamed, "SHARK!!!!," ripped me off his shoulders and threw me into the ocean as he ran in the direction of the beach. I believed him. I believed he'd my father had just thrown me to the sharks!

There was not one building block of rational belief that I could build upon as to why I was alive at all. I was four the first time I told someone I wished I could kill myself.

I saw ghosts. The wispy kind and the paralyzing kind. I played by myself all the time in the hauntings of our house that was once a hospital in the revolutionary war. It's so old we don't even know when it was built. We only know that it was built and standing by documentation in 1728. It was dark, windy, and something scary loomed in every crevice.

My parent's idea of fun was to scare the shit out of me. My dad brought deer heads into my bed after a day of hunting. Every time sirens went off, they told me the cops were coming for me and I needed to hide. They'd jump out when they knew I was most vulnerable. You know, that kind of scary fun.

I just did *not* understand why I was here, in this dark scary, confused fucked up place and I wanted out or at least a damn good reason.

I was a pawn in someone else's game, that much I knew. What I didn't know was who's hand it was that moved me. I had no say in the game being played or my place on it and the fingers that picked me up to move me around, always stung.

It felt like hell. I've been to hell in my dreams. I saw what the version of hell I would go to, if I slipped into that dimension of myself at my time of death, might look like. But, I *always* knew what it felt like.

"Burn in hell," was a phrase thrown around often.

It was our own little hell and everyone was trying to protect it somehow. From what, I'll never be able to understand, but I knew I'd wished I'd been the inadequate fawn that couldn't keep up and was left to die alone. Our hell was torture and we all knew it.

I was an exceptionally sensitive little girl who was given everything a kid could ever need physically. I was also robbed of everything I needed where it mattered most and I knew it early on.

The world didn't feel like home, but I was damn sure wherever home was, I wanted to go.

Bubbles. Moss. Especially water droplets in the shower. I looked at every molecule as a small world that feels, in a split second to them, like what our eternity feels to us. As in the difference between the life span of a butterfly and a human. If I stepped on it, I was certain I'd kill its forever. For as long as I could get away with, I'd sit down in the shower, staring at the water sliding down its walls wondering what life on that whole little world I was looking at, was like. Until I'd watch it crash to the floor in a natural fashion.

I learned quickly that the ones I tried to stop from merging with all of the others to their individual ending, died a premature death by my finger.

Everything had a life as far as I could see. Stuffed animals at the grocery store, the food I was afraid to eat, the walls of my room. The life in them always felt like it was watching me. Alone, I was certain that there were others with me, watching me, so I was always very good. Anything I did do maliciously, I silently apologized for, to whoever could hear me apologizing.

Never did I pull off the apology thing in real life during childhood though. I wasn't sorry. Everything as far as I could see, had a life filled with love and vibrancy, except the people who gave me life. A life they asked me to slave to, like shitty school teachers and "always right" doctors. They wanted me to be sorry. I never understand for what, so jaw-clenched, eyes swelling from resisting a well of tears, I refused to give it to them.

Shame. Guilt. Confusion. These were the attributes of my world. I sent prayers to other worlds in the life, right under our noses. I prayed each water droplet have a peaceful eternity where people loved each other, and where no one felt alone. I prayed they didn't have to be confused or hurt like the people in my world had to. I sent them love and envisioned the attributes in their world to be joyful.

My thoughts were my real world and I escaped to them often. For the very few years of my life I *didn't* spend berating myself with them, I *did* find happy connections in my escape. I'd talk to anyone who would listen because I knew someone was there, even if they didn't talk back with words.

I was certain every molecule here, were an eternity to a living, conscious world, but a split second to us. I was sure that our earth was a cell in a person who is universally bigger than us.

Imagine a black cut out version of a man with stars as cells. He's just some random guy living on some random world, living a random life and here we are, a measly cell that takes our own shit so seriously, thinking it's all hellish, and really we're just helping a dude digest his waste. I questioned whether the guy we lived in may be the cause of the hellish way people here see the world.

Maybe he's a guy that drinks bad beer, beats his wife, never ate vegetables, and buries cats up to their heads and runs them over with tractors for fun and that's why it feels so gross to live in his guts?

I was always afraid of my bad thoughts. Always. Likely because of the fact that my life was designed around effect and consequence, everything I did was scary. Especially think bad things, i.e., *I wish my mom were dead, that girl is a snob, I wish I could have a family like that.* Anything I wished, I always believed would come true, which totally sucked because I wished a lot of bad things. It was all I knew to do: to wish.

Wishing I had a family like *that* would send me on a spiral of thoughts, questioning what kind of family would want me, what if they beat me, wouldn't my mommy be upset if I left, what will she do with her life? Thinking some girl was a snob was the worst. I felt so ashamed of the thought, I'd hide from her because

I was certain she knew I thought it. Basically, the whole world could read my mind. I was certain if I even thought for a moment that I wished my mom would die, she would and I'd be to blame.

My grandmother told her mother she hated her when she was twelve and watched her die in a house fire hours later. I was pretty certain that's how life went.

I was gullible and confused; everything everyone told me, I believed. Worthless. Fat. Stupid. Spoiled.

Buffalo was my nickname, dedicated to my fat frame as an infant. I knew I wasn't a buffalo, though the only people who didn't call me Buffy were my school teachers. When my sister's friend first met me at age five, he said I was going to be a fox when I grew up. I hid behind my sister's legs and cried. For weeks I panicked, seeking reassurance that I wasn't going to grow up to turn into a fox.

I couldn't find a place in their truth, their lies, or anything in between.

My first seizure came when I was eighteen months old; pain-induced grand mal seizures. The kind that I fall over, convulse, choke on my tongue and always pissed myself because my heart slowed to an unrecognizable pulse. My mom assumed after I fell down the cellar steps into a concrete hole at the bottom, that my flailing about was nothing more than me having a temper tantrum, so she put me to bed.

I seized about once a week which transitioned to once a month for about twelve years.

Then, I began doing drugs.

The life story I spewed that day was colorfully decorated in stories of me stealing cars at the age of twelve, losing my virginity to my first love at age thirteen, my first stint in rehab at age fourteen, you know, normal adolescent stuff. Or so I thought.

My parents just hid their keys so I wouldn't take their cars and only totally lost their shit on me once when I had way too many kids sleep over and stole their car with all of them in it. We certainly put our guardian angels to serious work those days.

When they found out I was doing drugs and having sex (because my sister told them), they sat me down in an almost too-calm fashion. They let me know they knew what I was doing and that I shouldn't be doing it, but what was *most* important is I keep my grades up and dress proper so I didn't look like the whore I was. Then they let my boyfriend move in with us. He came from an abusive, negligent family and I begged my parents to help him. So they did because I was a spoiled brat who got whatever I wanted.

I was nine the first time my mother bought me a diary and nine the first time she locked herself in a bathroom reading it while I punched on the outside of the door begging for her to give it back. I wrote I liked a boy. She sobbed from the inside of the bathroom, screaming, "My daughter's a whore! My daughter's a whore!" Naturally, I never wrote again.

I got suspended from school pretty consistently, which was awesome for me. The in-school suspension ladies whose job it was to sit with us were always pretty good at seeing my innocence under my bull shit. They talked to me like I was human and not like the savage I had become to the world.

Still, I never did my work for two reasons: One, no one was ever patient enough to actually teach me without screaming, so I shut down at anything academic, and two, because by the time I was old enough to get suspended, I had a point to prove and it was a big, *"Fuck you!"*

For whatever reason, one of the in-school suspension ladies took it upon herself to write a self-addressed letter to my mother and tell her I was an amazing writer, encouraging my mother to consider fostering that in me.

My seventh grade English teacher saw me. She saw me to my core. She put up with my bull shit with a smile knowing I would never truly cross her. I didn't threaten her like I threatened others. People were weary of me because of my reputation at being a careless, ruthless, reckless trouble maker. My mother constantly reiterated, "You don't want to make a name for yourself!" but I already had one.

My teacher was old and soft, and she understood something I didn't think the world did. She understood that I was hiding behind my actions. My actions were a manner of self-preservation from the threats of the world. I'd never hurt anyone, but I made damn sure they knew I could if I wanted to.

No one had ever told me that anyone believed in me. My mother often said, "You are smarter than your father and I put together, but you're too stupid to use it," in a backhanded attempt to give me a compliment about her belief in me. She especially didn't tell me about the inspired letter from the In-school-suspension lady.

My seventh grade English teacher though was curious about what I could create. She believed in me and though she never told me, she showed me in her quiet, restrained way of guiding me to who she knew I could be, rather than demean me for being who I was.

I wanted to be a version of her to everyone I met. I wanted to show them I saw them the way she showed me she saw me. She was also a literature teacher and writer, so organically, my inclination was to hope to be a literature teacher when I grew up.

She handed me the gift of my gift. She let it be ok that I was what I was and that I wanted to express myself at all. Not only that, she'd correct me without labelling me as an ignoramus.

My experience with her, sparked a curiosity in me that never left. The year before, I had almost failed sixth grade just to prove the point that no one could disempower me into doing anything I didn't want to do a day longer. The only reason I passed was because my math teacher hated me so much she gave me a D so she didn't have to see me again the following year. She as much as told my parents that. Then my English teacher showed up with some ideas that tickled my fancy. Ones that made me come alive without hurting myself to feel anything at all.

High school was a blur of drugs, hippies, festivals and psychedelic insights. I slept with three boys in the duration of my high school. Spoken like an expert in the bait and catch department, not because I couldn't sleep with more. I declared that if anyone was going to touch my body, or be inside of my heart, or soul, it wasn't going to be the hands or cocks of another. No one could hurt me but me. I partied hard, watching over friends, mothering them through drunken emotional fits and had their backs in belligerent arguments. Really though, I was just so dirtied and ashamed that the thought of my body being exposed in any way at all, was absolutely disgusting and I wouldn't want to subject anyone at all to my grossness. I only slept with people I deeply wanted to trust. In retrospect, not too keenly.

My dad had a serious affair he wanted to leave my mother for. He made all kinds of promises that we'd move out and wouldn't be under her reign anymore. I deeply wanted to believe him.

She'd leave when she was under-appreciated. With a car packed to the brim with her belongings, she'd drive away. I'd sit out on the apartment steps next to our house, smoking cigarettes, timing how long it would take her to be back screaming, "I'm not going anywhere! This is my house!" Usually, it'd be within ten minutes.

Though I found my mother's frantic outbursts somewhat comical as my father and I stared at each other quietly with smirks that swore a shared witness to her insanity, it must've been just as confusing for her as it was for me.

My parent's relationship ended the day I was born, according to my father. My mother devoted her life to me. She used me as her Barbie and a pawn for her own emotional projections, but she gave up a life she once had for the "sake" of her child because that's "just what parents do." I was the cause of their separation and I was reminded of it often. I was frequently reminded that I should be thanking my mother for giving up her life for me. She swore up and down, that if it wasn't for her, I wouldn't have a father at all, but that if I wasn't born, they may still have a decent relationship.

She pushed him away at every turn. He'd try to engage and she'd either resentfully give in ~ though not often, or push him away, hard. As she did me.

So, when my father disclosed his affair to me on a drunken stint while we partied in the woods, having a philosophical conversation about love, lust, and belonging, I too, drunk, stumbled out of the woods a sobbing mess. I had no idea at the time why I was crying, but that night, after I drove us all out of the woods (driving stick shift for the first time), I pulled into my driveway and my father's girlfriend on the side of his *actual* girlfriend (set aside his *actual* wife) jumped out of the car with her five year old daughter. Yes, we were drunk driving with children in the car. Many children actually. I was one of them.

Anyway, my mom ran down the yard bitching that my father let me drive at age fourteen, and I overheard his girlfriend on the side of his *girlfriend* whisper in her daughter's ear, "Do you want Elias to be your new Daddy?"

That sentence lit me on fire! For years!

Actually, it somehow grew inside of me rendering me paralyzed over the course of a couple years. My father's willingness to disclose his secret, solidified his love for me in my mind. I would hold it for him and this would prove that he really did love me, he was just always absent because he truly couldn't stand my mother. But those words, "Do you want Elias to be your new Daddy?" blowing every ounce of possibility of ever having my own father to myself, ripped me apart. There I was, feeling solid by this secret we shared only to be blown away by the very stark reality that this secret we shared was not benefiting me at all. In fact, his girlfriend on the side of his girlfriend was now standing in the way of my union and on top of that, placing her beautifully innocent five year old in a position to be of threat to my security. It was ironically also the first night in my entire life I saw my own parents kiss.

He didn't end up with his girlfriend on the side, but our shared secret did open the doors for him to tell me of his true love who he longed for me to know. She was married too. I met her a few times. She was decent.

After a week when my mother and I were both out of the house (me in summer camp and her on work travel), my father told me that his girlfriend's husband and he got into a fist fight when they were caught making out at a bar. She was given an ultimatum by her husband in that moment. She chose my father and since we weren't home, she came to our house and slept in my mother's bed. As much as I coddled his lust, that was too far for me.

Here I insert the part that over these two years of harboring his secret, I had been absent from school more times than I can count and gained about thirty five pounds. My suicidal depressions were exhausting. Staring at the wall was the best I could muster up. I ate and slept. I rarely cried. I was too angry to cry.

People at school were making fun of me for carrying around my new friend, fat, everywhere I went. My friend fat, of course, was unbearable for my mother to stomach. To clarify the severity of my food addiction, I got a job at a donut shop and I kid you not, every single night I'd eat at least a dozen donuts as a fourth meal. So, I turned to puking and diet pills.

I hated puking as it was, but to be thin enough for my mother's love without bursting all of this fat and shame away by spewing my father's secret, bulimia and diet pills felt like the only way to keep some sort of fucked up balance I knew they needed me to keep so they didn't have to look at themselves.

I was their buffer. They needed me to be a *problem* so they didn't have to look at their own. On my last drive to outpatient rehab when I was either going to go home that night or to inpatient rehab, my father said, "I don't know if you're still using but if you are, I cannot be in the house alone with your mother. Say whatever you need to say to come home." I was fourteen with the weight of their unhappiness floating through every fiber of my being. I knew what I needed to do. I lied and an hour later, drove home with my savior, sure he'd be thankful I was now the one saving him.

I overheard my parent's short lived conversation from the bathroom as I stuck my finger down my throat on my mother's behalf.

"Where's Stac?" my father asked.

"Upstairs making herself puke."

"She better not be!" he said, and they left it at that.

That was the last day I puked. Knowing my mother knew what I was doing so nonchalantly and she allowed it to be, just so I could look good for the world she wanted to fit into, enraged me enough to let myself be fat for vengeance. So, I did.

I hated food, but I ate it all the time. I hated being made fun of for gaining weight. I hated my body. I hated my life. I hated everything, except my dad. Somehow, I always held some shiny silver speck of aliveness in my dark green heart that lit up with my father's presence.

I had boyfriends on and off, but hated myself so much that if they loved me, or even liked me, I believed they were weak. I almost orgasmed once and stopped myself out of embarrassment. I had better luck orgasming as a seven year old playing anatomy class with the girls up the street, before shame smashed into orgasms like a bulldozer and took every sensation of release right out of them.

I also stayed in an on and off relationship with my first love, the boy my parents allowed to live with us for two years when we were thirteen to fifteen for the entirety of my middle and high school experience.

I knew he loved me, but I couldn't understand it. He got another girl pregnant when we were in high school which was incredibly hard for me *(and him and her)*. I also slept with him again while she was pregnant with his baby which made me feel like an even bigger loser than I already felt like. That night I laid on my bedroom floor after he left, listening to Sinead O'Connor's "Nothing Compares to You" in a puddle of my own tears, until I cried myself to sleep. I loved him sure, but this wanna-be-sad fit came from a deeper knowing that I had just become my father. I fucked someone else's lover. Even at age fifteen, I wondered what I'd really done it for. One more tally to check off for digging my claws into the spine of a man just because I could, I suppose.

I perceived my mother to be weak and stupid for letting all of this go on under her nose, so my mindset was to always be in the know. I observed and listened, but I observed and listened with my heart more than with meaningless words of fakers. Quite honestly, as much as my actions of lashing out may have annoyed the world, the world annoyed me a hell of a lot more than I annoyed it, I assure you.

I didn't want to be weak, perceived as weak, or smell of weakness because honestly, I didn't trust myself with the scent of weakness. I felt like I'd crush it just because I wished I could or because that's what I was taught to do with weakness. Maybe not even because I *wanted* to but because weakness was associated with the feeling of being crushed and I didn't want to be close to that feeling. Weakness of any kind may envelop me into a black hole like my mother's blind rages. I'd gobble it or it would gobble me.

The girl my boyfriend had gotten pregnant, had at one time been my friend. I stood as she begged me, with her huge pregnant belly, never to hold her baby. The thought of her baby in my arms, crushed her. I didn't care if she hated me with her *own* anger. I was used to that. But, I did care if I hurt her.

She taught me a lot about the boundaries of the heart and womanhood that day. I was fifteen, but I honored her bravery in the vulnerability of her honesty. I never held her child.

I was with him for two years after she was born and never came around when she was around. Not because I didn't love his daughter or want to know her, but because his daughter's mother showed me in her tears that day in the hallways of high school, my first witness of the tenderness of a mothers love and I wanted nothing to come in between her daughter's opportunity to keep that, not even my *own* love. I wanted to keep her connection to her daughter as sacred as I could because I wanted to believe it existed.

I was a floater. The athletes probably thought I was fat. The fat people probably thought I was gorgeous. The gorgeous people thought I was a stoner. The stoners, well, they knew I was a stoner, but probably thought I was catty. The catty people probably thought I was a bull and the bullish people never really fucked with me, which was good because I didn't want them to see that I wasn't a bull. I was a lone wolf of sorts. Always on the periphery, showing up, dropping out. One thing that I can say is I was the leader of my kind of floaters. I found everyone who didn't fit in, in all the same ways I didn't, and we made ourselves a safety net.

I never made sense to myself and never really tried to. I sincerely believed I'd be dead by fifteen. When I was sixteen and still alive, I sat in the back of the car of a man who got his lip sewn back together after the fist of my first love split it open for taking me into dangerous places to get illegal things when I was very young. His lip was healed for months at this point, but he hated me quietly. We were wasted. I was in the back, sandwiched between two men, on a very windy road. I watched the speedometer of his car raise to ninety-five miles per hour. I closed my eyes and heard a voice whisper in my left ear, "Don't close your eyes. If we're going to die, don't you want to know how? Just look."

I opened my eyes. That question never left me. My entire life had been a life walking around scared, with parentally induced terrors and circumstantial traumas. My head had gone through two windshields and I'd been in a car accident that was so bad my entire trunk and back seat had been smashed into my front seat. My guardian angels had always been conspiring on my behalf.

His question, "Don't you wanna know how you're going to die?" flipped the script that my *fear* was in the hands of my parents and the world. Rather, the possibility that it was a personal choice to hold fear in my hands, hold my hands close to my chest and look right down at it, completely in my control. We had lost plenty of our mutual friends to drug and alcohol related deaths, but nothing stopped us. We acted unafraid, but I knew we were just challenging how very afraid we all were.

I didn't know exactly what I feared, but I did fear everything and I also feared nothing. I feared the silent stares at the wall in hopeless depression, the food I didn't want to eat, but knew I would, the line laced with something I didn't expect, being a nobody, being a somebody, being found out (that there was nothing to find out), the bottomless void of the human condition, I feared simple people for their stupidity, and audacious people for their bravery. I feared me. I feared the cops were coming for me, and that every bad thought I think about my mother would come true. I feared I would always be hot and cold in relationships and dig my fingernails deeply into the skin of those more vulnerable than I, digging up chunks of flesh on them, the way my mother often did on my own arms. I feared that everything wrong with the world was my fault because I couldn't fix it, so I geared up with armor thick enough to wall *in* my fear, and *out* the world. I didn't trust what I would do to people from a world I felt so violated by.

My actions actually did drive someone to their death. It actually happened.

When you grow up with a couple hundred people in your class, even if we don't know them, we know them. A friend ran up to me laughing, to tell me that a kid had poured a poisonous chemical with no scent and no taste into someone's drink. Two people drank out of it and both were now vomiting uncontrollably up and down the hallways. The teachers and authorities that called 911 assumed they had accidentally gotten it under their fingernails. They took lighter measures than necessary under that assumption. No one who knew was willing to tell. I knew there was a possibility that they'd die if the authorities didn't know the extent of their ingestion. I told on a kid I had known my entire school life for putting poison in someone's drink. Two lives saved from aggressive stomach pumping because of this tattle tale. A couple years later, he killed himself. Of course, I blamed myself.

It was never enough to just be enough. I learned that when I was very young, so I went to college with dreams of intellectuals, hippies and parties which is exactly what I got. However, I also got pharmaceuticals way too readily. Heavy pharmaceuticals. I met the second love of my life, who happened to be a woman, but I felt too much like a violator to physically be with her. My feelings of being a perpetrator probably come from every line I've ever been thrown that suggested I instigated or asked for any and all violations that I endured.

One semester in, after a drug bust that almost got me expelled, I was given the option to go back to rehab while I was still in school, or come home. I secretly did want to get clean.

My roommate held my face on many nights, in a nodding out stupor, holding a mirror to me to show what I looked like on the shit. I knew I'd never get clean while I was at school only because, as much as I wanted to get clean, I also wanted to use. Coming from situations like this, I knew my only fix was to get away from half of what I wanted. So I did. I dropped out, left my second love on a snowy February afternoon, and headed back…to the hell I came from.

I brought my college boyfriend, who also happened to be my weed dealer, with me. He pulled a hair out of the mole on my face once, so I believed he loved me because he didn't judge me. We traveled to my hell with the intent to better our lives.

My entire life as I knew it had been resisting my resistance of the hell from which I had come. Here I was, returning to the heart of it at a war with myself with the intention of making peace. Peace doesn't come from war. I didn't know that yet. I didn't know peace didn't need to be reined in and conquered. It only needed me to give up my resistance, so it could come.

What that long snowy drive home was about to teach me was that if we don't take care of every sign, every symptom, every intuitive nudge that moves through us, the universe will give us a royal, and not so swift, kick right in the ass to get our attention. We can listen to the call of our own darkness as a beacon *from* the light that has come to save us from the hell we believe we're living in. Or, we can listen to the call of darkness as a beacon of proof that our own hell is the only way we'll ever know ourselves while we're alive.

The Low Road.

"If only our eyes saw souls instead of bodies, how very different our ideals of beauty would be."

—Unknown

I SINCERELY ANTICIPATED death as a teenager, so these college years were very unexpected. I never planned my future. I never dreamed up schemes about being a boss one day, or being a mother, or wearing an ivory dress on my wedding day. Admittedly, my most perpetual thoughts always had me succumb to my own death (whether it was that day or fifty years from that day).

There was less access to hard drugs, so my liver function was probably cleaner than it'd been in years. I'd had a job since the day my working papers came through at fifteen. Always with the intention of getting "out" of some form of perceived hell. Again, I wanted out. I did what I thought I had to do to get me out and keep me clean.

I landed a night job taking care of adults in a vegetative state. I bought myself my teenage dream car, a Jeep Wrangler and my college boyfriend bought me my dream companion, a Siberian Husky. Working with adults in diapers, caring for my boon companion, and busting my ass to pay off my Jeep, brought a sense of clarity to the frailty of life. It brought clarity to the not-so-fucking-serious parts of life that'd haunted me before.

Up until that point, life happened to me. People projected things onto me and I owned their projections as if they were true. I stayed hidden in a small pocket of myself, tucked somewhere inside of my left hip, and came out only to ward off the demons that got too close to my cozy, comfy, cave inside of myself with their attacks on the only safe space I'd been successful at preserving. I'd never played. I'd never asserted my truest desires. My entire life had been one of hiding from the world and dodging bullets of sarcasm, condescension, judgment, and ridicule.

Here I was, happening to life. I was responsible for the lives of vulnerable humans though some of them weighed a hundred pounds more than I did. Strangely, my bosses trusted me to be gentle, to be loving, to be attentive, to these voiceless, non-communicative people.

I'd never been shown physical touch, or affection for my own perfect right to just be loved because I'm worth loving. Naturally, I didn't understand the nurturance or affection thing but I did understand the things people didn't say. I've always listened with an ear to the unsaid. Those were the things I tended to honor most.

These people in vegetative states, were showing me with their eyes, who they were. I swore to myself to honor the voiceless by giving them the voice I always wanted the world to hear from me. I'd let them show me exactly who they were, having no doubt that what I couldn't see about them, but only know, is that they are big and beautiful, perfect beings on the inside that were just as aware as I was, that this whole thing was just some seemingly planned-to-our-demise shit show, but that on the inside, we were secretly celebrating our safety in a raging fairy-forrest dance party with a ton of our fairy friends.

In genuine connection as their keeper, I was certain that we went to the same place when we escaped. I'd decided I'd only see them the way I'd see them were they not trapped in the walls of their immobile bodies, but as free, frolicking, dancers at the same celebration of freedom party I was on the road to. That's how I saw them, which is not an easy task when you're changing someone's shitty diaper. They were just a larger version of the water droplets I wondered about what kinds of spiraling, gorgeous, joyous worlds were going on inside of.

Innocent. Worth loving. Just because.

One of the residents was a gorgeous woman exactly my age, confined to a crib. I heard her crying in her room at night. I'd go in, sit, stare through her bright green eyes, and hold space for her to cry. She was trapped, physically, mentally, emotionally, but she stared at me with eyes that talked through her tears. Her pleas for freedom were no different than mine, but her stare wasn't indifferent to who had the potential to get out of our individually designed hells.

I wanted reprieve for these people, and for myself. At the time, I swore their only reprieve was death, and so was mine.

Her eyes let me know which one of us had the resources to get out of our hell, without wasting our potential and I didn't want to be alive, in a free body, feeling as trapped as she was. One of us at least, could find our way out to find peace in the world we were born into.

Every question about why God would keep them alive, what our purpose on the planet is, why they were in my life and why I was getting paid to take care of their essentially lifeless bodies came up. I aligned with Dr. Kevorkian's philosophies, but they couldn't talk to give informed consent.

Mammy Mae (I wish I could write her name the way I say her full name. I know she still hears it ringing through the cosmos) silently gifted me with the grace of feeling the essence of someone's Spirit in its flow and its absence from her. You know those pictures of orbs sitting right outside of someone's body at the moment of their death which is supposed to confirm there is life after life? Well, I didn't need a camera to prove to me that Miss Mammy Mae was in constant entrance and exit from her body. She was different than the others. She had mastered a way to come into her body to enjoy the good, but leave, traveling into the ethers with her divine friends a majority of the time. Her presence was palpable even in her quiet, and her absence was palpable even with a pumping pulse.

The time to reflect in the quiet of their agony, their methods for reprieve, their fully committed life to being completely purposeless to the naked eye, deemed to be a very introspective time in my life. I needed them and their silent teachings, more than they needed me to roll them in avoidance of bed sores and to wipe their asses. It doesn't matter how comfortable our bed is. If we lay in it long enough, we'll end up with bed sores. This is a metaphor for life. Comfortable in my discomfort for far too long, this is what they taught me.

I had since left the world of playing with my invisible friends and of being guided by my angels, and seeing ghosts. That world terrified me because I was alone in it. Sure, my family saw the ghosts I saw, but they still played it off like we should be skeptical even after my father came into the kitchen to see the cabinets all opening and closing at the same time, *on their own.*

When my college boyfriend and I walked into my parents' house in the middle of the night, it was undeniable what we both heard and he was not someone inclined to believe in the unseen.

A baby crying is what we heard. Loudly. Clear as anything. We looked at each other and shifted our weight to look into the living room to see if my nephew had been sleeping over, but no one was there. In the morning, we asked. No baby had been in the house.

I was eighteen years old and secretly it was the first thing in my life I knew without a doubt. It was the first thing I wouldn't let anyone steal from me with their doubts, their insecurities, or their fears. I didn't tell a soul, but I knew what we heard and what it meant.

A memory continued to surface after that night. I was fourteen, brushing my teeth beside a campfire, staring across the flames as the sun peeked through the wood line at the break of day. We had been up all night, partaking in psychedelic experiences. As others were waking, we were contemplating where and when our heads would hit a soft pillow. My friend sitting across the fire yelled out to a passerby walking the trail, "Hey, have you seen Averiel?" I was pretty content to brush my teeth and wallow in my tiredness, but the sound of that name excited me. I wanted to meet someone with the name Averiel. I envisioned his energy. I felt his strength, his uniqueness, his laid back willfulness. I turned my head to see this man who was being sought after, but he was nowhere. Actually, he never existed.

My friend had said, "Gabriel."

That cry meant he was coming. I knew four years later, I was about to meet the essence that had made its way to me the morning of brushing my teeth in the woods.

A month came, and so did a positive pregnancy test.

My boyfriend said we could do whatever I wanted. My father said, "How could you be so God damn stupid?" and went into the yard to shoot birds as his outlet. My mother pleaded with me to get an abortion.

That day in her living room, she told me my life would be over. No man would ever love me because I have a child. I'd never be able to take care of it. I'd never be able to move out and have a good life. After all, I was technically a college dropout, newly clean junkie, directionless eighteen year old, naive, senseless child myself. That day in her living room was also the first decision I'd made for myself. Ever.

I told her it didn't matter what she thought, feared, or wanted, I was keeping my baby. Period.

For reasons I can only chalk up to being caused by my willingness to surrender the idea that I or my parents knew shit about life, the world began opening spiritual avenues only those who've traveled on them could comprehend. Simply, I was beginning to see that no one knew shit about anything. I began to undress myself from the clothes of stories my parents dressed me in.

At the time, Miss Mammy Mae had a profuse sweating problem. Within seconds out of nowhere, she'd sweat so badly, we'd have to change her entire outfit. I mean, she was drenched as if someone had run her through an indoor car wash, zero to sixty in ten seconds. In honor of helping Miss Mammy Mae, my work afforded me a reiki class in hopes of seizing her sweats.

During my first reiki class, we were asked to close our eyes for a meditation. Now, I was not a meditator. And closing my eyes with other people in the room was pretty much likened to me being so trust worthy I'd probably get shot or slapped the second I closed them, so the mere act of closing my eyes made me feel vulnerable beyond what my pride wanted to allow.

I forced myself to trust the people I'd been told were wack-jobs my whole life, who sat with their eyes closed not even contemplating that I could be some psycho who was about to steal from them or slit their throats. When I closed my eyes, I had a memory of being twelve years old with a group of friends in my living room. We were laying our hands on each other, playing with the molecules of air between our hands and bodies. We were also high and the only people we trusted.

I let that memory settle in as a reminder that whatever new-age thing we were doing, had an ancient home in my bones long before any facilitators in a room brought it to my attention.

I knew this room wasn't full of wack-jobs and text books, it was full of me and full of what I had come for.

Cross my heart, on the mornings I'd reiki Miss Mammy Mae for even just two minutes, she'd go an entire day without having a sweating episode.

Reiki sessions and ten dollars an hour were perfect tools for the time, but I was certain there was more to quench my thirst for life. Attempting to avoid settling like so many statistical stories of teenage mothers in my shoes, I revved up my engine for full focused academia as a stepping stone to having some sort of advantage in my unfolding destiny of motherhood.

I enrolled at a local college because I believed it would buy me time and give me some empowered direction and intellectual stimulation apart from the case study my boyfriend and I were secretly doing on my family. School. And work. Full time.

Four months into my pregnancy, I found a bump on my vagina. Mind you, every test I had taken had resulted in perfectly healthy feedback. No viruses, no blood issues, no sexually transmitted diseases.

My obstetrician ordered a surgery to remove a genital wart the next month. Every fear I'd ever had about my vagina being disgusting or used goods was made manifest in this conversation. I'd slept with less people than pretty much everyone I knew and had only heard of one person who'd been diagnosed with an STD. I stared at my boyfriend in my obstetrician's office. He shrugged his shoulders and mouthed, "I'm sorry."

We thought it would end there. I thought that was the worst case scenario so I stewed in anger at the injustice I felt being placed upon my body. STD's were for whores. I was a druggy, not a whore.

Unfair.

Questionable Legacy.

"If you would not be forgotten as soon as you are dead, either write some-thing worth reading, or do something worth writing."

—*Benjamin Franklin*

AN EMERGENCY CALL came for me at work a few days after my surgery. My fa-ther's mother, who'd lived next door to me my entire life was on her death bed. It was time.

I left work and met my family at her bedside. I gave her reiki and said a prayer, ending it with possibly the first real tears I'd shed in years. There was a dry spell of my emotions. An apathy to the terrible *and* the great and I was a walled up zombie observing it. But, in this moment, I asked her if she'd be my child's guardian angel and the flood gates of my pent up sorrows and dreams and wishes came crashing down.

She transitioned to spirit right then and there. My grandmother died in my hands and it was nothing short of the most peaceful thing I'd witnessed up until that point in my life.

It struck me to consider her legacy as I laid in bed, letting years of emo-tion move through me. I didn't know her. I essentially lived with this woman by my side for eighteen years, but a majority of those years were riddled with Alzheimers. She was old, and I was young, and we'd never found a way to con-nect. I suppose we both tried, but she was weird and dirty and I was lost.

She bought me a rabbit once under my mother's strict orders not to, even though it lived at her house. When the rabbit died a few weeks later, I was devastated. Ashamed, listening to my mother berate my grandmother for trying to do something good for me, I eavesdropped on my mother's lecture.

She also let me store all of my water spider pets in her living room. She was interesting. She had six kids. She loved babies. She smelled terrible. She was a hoarder. I mean, really, really bad. Basically though, all I knew of her was that she was vulnerable, marked by the times she'd meet my friends outside in the middle of the night trying to clean up water that wasn't there, that she was sure had spilled on the front porch. A symptom of her disease.

She shit herself at most dinners we ate together. She swore she was religious, but hated Catholics. She implemented a rainy day fund at her house. Every day it rained, she'd put a dollar in a jar to donate it, trying to make good vibes out of dreary days. All in all, she tried I suppose.

But, I couldn't pinpoint exactly what her legacy was. Sure, she had kids, a husband, a house, a long life, but…for what? As far as I could see, I'd known my grandmother to be half dead like every other person I'd grown up around. No one, but us would know she ever even existed. A legacy of merely existing was not a legacy I wanted to be a part of. The point of her life rattled my cage. I just couldn't see what it was. Like factory farming, we appeared to be born, just to die.

I was raised to succeed. That was proof of my worth. Being enough was never enough. Just being on the planet was an inconvenience to everyone. It was made clear to me the only reason I was being raised was so I could succeed in a world I didn't feel I asked to be born into.

Then, why was my grandmother ever alive? What was the point in succeeding falsely if it just leads to death?

A motto I heard pretty much daily was, "Life sucks, and then you die." And that's exactly what I saw.

A day after her funeral was settled, I just turned nineteen years old, was five months pregnant, a newly clean junkie, diagnosed with an STD, directionless, in a relationship I knew wouldn't last, pretty much friendless, and contemplating purpose and legacy and spirit on my parent's couch. I stared at the blue and white striped wall paper when the call came.

My obstetrician's assistant called. What felt like a slow motion movie she bluntly relayed, "Stacy, It's Janet. Listen hon, I'm going to give you a referral for an oncologist."

Me, nineteen and naive, "What's an oncologist?"

"A cancer specialist. The results of your surgery are showing pre-cancer cells. It's looking like you have vulvar dysplasia. It's pretty rare, but your oncologist can tell you all about it. I know this isn't the news you were expecting, but the doctor will fill you in."

I wrote down the information like I was writing a love note to my middle school boyfriend. Nervous, intrigued to know how he'd take it, uncertain of why I was writing it in the first fucking place.

"Ok. Bye."

Stationary, I stared harder at the white and blue stripes of the wall paper across the room. An alien thought kept ruminating over itself through my head: "If you're not living, you're dying."

I knew I hadn't fully lived a day of my life. I knew I'd always been dying or hiding in avoidance of the reality that the real me was dying on the inside. This moment was a reaffirmation that life was pointless because it just leads to *this* kind of conversation.

You know, the kind of conversation that says, "You're creating the most important thing in your entire life *(a baby)* and now it's going to be taken from you just like every other twinkle of real life you've ever been curious about but never got to touch. It's going to be taken from you with a swift slap right across your face just like anything else you've ever secretly wanted. Worse yet, in the end, it'll still be your mother whose guilted you because she had to care for you your entire life, who will pick up the pieces of your un-lived life yet again because you, my friend, will soon know true death while she martyrs your long awaited absence."

My life was a carrot dangling in front of my starving soul.

Picture this: A stage. An audience. A glass box big enough to fit about 20 people, with a ceiling too high for even the tallest person to reach on the stage.

In that glass box is a naked girl curled up in a fetal position in the back right hand corner as to not be ridiculed by the audience for every imperfection she possesses, while vying to get angry enough or brave enough to shatter that glass, finding her way out into a life un-slaved. That glass was my life and it felt like every person in it was suffocating me in that stupid box. All I ever wanted to do was shatter that glass and watch it come down like confetti, breaking my body's skin into a bloody show just to feel something real.

My life had always felt like I was behind a glass that I could *see* through to the other side but never actually *get* through. Alone. Desolate. Confusing. A tease.

Somehow, this phone call, somehow, the thought, "If you aren't living, you're dying," gave me the personal audacity to stand on my two feet and say *"Fuck this! I'm done dying."*

For a minute, I teared up at the uncertainty of losing my life, of losing my unborn baby, of leaving a world I'd not yet learned to love. But after the first sixty-two seconds of planning my own funeral, I felt something inside me shift. When I stood up from the couch that day, I had a *fullness* of determination I'd never known. It wasn't like the *emptiness* of the determination I'd had as a little girl visioning my own funeral with spitefully mischievous intent, wondering if they'd notice me more if I were dead.

If I had a choice to be any superpower, it'd be *invisibility*. If I was going to be invisible, I wanted it to be on my terms. I was *too much* for someone else every time I let myself be seen, so I retreated twelve steps into my psychic basement to hide when I met life too far on the outskirts of my own boundaries. Too much to be *invisible* and *not enough* to be loved, I decided in that moment that I'd *fill* the rest of my life with what I loved, rather than try to *get rid* of what I don't. It wasn't until much later I learned how profound that last sentence is.

Holding out her open hand with closed fingers in my direction, my later-in-life lesbian love asked, "If I put water in my hand as it is, how will I keep it in?" Obviously, the answer is that she'd have to keep her hand open, cupping the water in order to keep it. Let's translate *keep* here, to *cherish*. If she closed her hand, the water would squeeze right through her fingers, leaving her with a closed hand and no opportunity to obtain more water. I was that clenched fist, unopened, who'd closed myself up in order to get rid of what I didn't want, and in doing so, I closed myself off from everything I actually *did* want. Closed is closed, to everything. Open is open, to everything.

The second decision I ever made on my own, posed to be the first decision I'd ever made for myself, *by myself.* This was not a decision for the sake of someone else at a time I deemed everyone other than me, worthy of a great life. Hence, my innocent, unborn baby. This was a decision for the sake of my own destiny. A decision that required just an ounce of belief that I may actually be important enough to invest in.

My entire family was already living like the dead. I was raised into an undeniable fear that penetrated any risks I may have taken at learning to love and learning to live. I decided that day that if nothing more, I would organize my life as such that even if I had to video tape myself speaking to my unborn child for every missed birthday while I was away on death leave, that my child wouldn't question what my legacy was when he thought about my absence.

I decided that day to become fully alive in the time I had left, to offer my child the only and greatest blessing I could: the opportunity to truly *know* its mother. Not just what I *did*, or what my life was like, but to give my child the opportunity I myself, didn't yet have. *To know me.* Not my fear, not my apparent free spirit based on rebellion, but me without all of the layers of social shit I'd bought into since the day I came, unwanted, into the world.

Putting me in touch with my creative forces, the life inside of me was teaching me that not one damn person on the planet was going to come save me or my kid. If I wanted to become fully alive in this one chance at life we'd been given together, I needed to begin creating on the outside as well.

I knew, I was the person I had been longing for. I knew it was my time to save, and it wasn't every innocent stuffed animal in the store that was as unwanted as I was I'd be saving. It was me.

The memory that resonated most in that moment was feeling the pit in my stomach as my mother stood at my bedroom door and threw me square across the room from my door, onto my bed, slamming the door behind her. I was naked and cold in our old drafty house. I may have been four years old when it happened, but my stomach dropped about once a day for my entire life the way it did the night I cried myself to sleep, naked, alone, confused, and praying to God (who was my only friend) to please help. How I wanted help, I wasn't sure, but I knew we (my parents and I) needed it.

This time, I wanted to own that pitiful sensation instead of letting it own me the way it did each time I heard my mother's footsteps walking up the stairs.

Every time I touched that pit in my stomach, in situations that weren't even relatable to it, I was sending a call out to the Universe, a prayer to God, to please come and save me.

That day, I decided I would.

I'd save me.

Low On The Low Road.

"The dark night of the soul is when you have lost the flavor of life but have not yet gained the fullness of divinity. So it is that we must weather the dark time, the period of transformation when what is familiar has been taken away and the new richness is not yet ours."

—*Ram Dass*

IT'S A BOLD statement to say that I know what female genital mutilation feels like. Six months pregnant, the doctors burned off layers and layers of the outside of my vagina. Think Mars being hit with fifty burning craters leaving deep seething holes where the craters hit. Once my vagina was likened to earth. Watery, fluid, molten, but now, it was Mars with flaming craters. Visually, it looked exactly as I've just described. Black burning craters, everywhere.

It was no accident my vagina had issues. I spent my entire life shaming, judging, and hating that part of me, and I knew it was communicating in return. It had manifested what I'd always feared. By now, there was no doubt in my mind why I slept with less people than my friends and ended up with an STD. They were unapologetic about their rendezvous. Meanwhile, I was guilting and shaming myself for each infrequent sexcapade.

The lesson I was taught but rebelled against the most was that a woman's body was to please a man. Nothing more, nothing less. So, every time I used it as a forfeit of my own integrity for the sake of someone else's pleasure, I ridiculed and shamed myself for having *given in*. I didn't even like sex. Truly. I did it because I believed I had to in order to be loved and in turn I ended up hating myself. My vagina was now saying, "Hey, fuck you too bitch. It's about time you love me. I'm gonna make you love me but, I'm gonna make the process hurt because apparently hurt is how you learn best."

What I didn't expect was what came next. The first time I remember my mother actively staying with me through something in an engaged way, was the night of my surgery. I've never felt pain like that in my life. I couldn't pull one apart from the other. What grew on top of my black burning craters were red, opening blisters. For two days, I suspected this was part of the healing process. I couldn't sleep, sit or stand. All I could do was scream. Two unbearable days later, we found out in an emergency visit with my oncologist that I was having a herpes outbreak.

My oncologist suggested I take a serious look at my relationship with my boy-friend because I didn't have herpes when he tested me weeks before. I couldn't leave now anyway. I was indeed, proven, used goods.

Herpes, HPV, vulvar cancer, junkie, teenage mom, bulimic, college drop out. If those days had hashtags it would've been summed up by #notwinning. Not winning at all.

During one of our most infamous fights my boyfriend sent me a message loud and clear. He said, "I don't give a fuck if I never see this kid. I'll make damn sure you don't! You're a junkie." I screamed and sobbed so hard outside, in nothing but overalls until I fell on the ground in a pregnant exhausted stupor of hyperventilation. He picked me up, put me into bed, and left anyway.

It's not like I trusted I could lean on him as safety through my struggles. I knew it was me and this kid. Getting my shit together proved to be the most terri-fying thought there was to choose from, while also being the absolute only choice.

Everything I was learning moved me in the direction of natural healing, natural living, and natural parenting, including natural childbirth. Due to my re-cent surgery, STD outbreaks and my lifelong pain induced seizures, my doctors convinced me to get a C-section which I willfully resented.

I grew up in a house that felt inferior to the man. Anyone with letters behind their name was automatically perceived as being brighter than my parents (by my parents) hence brighter than me. Though my first seizure came very shortly after my MMR shot, no one made a connection that vaccines and my body don't mix. Actually, before my parents stepped up their game about my seizures, they took me to a doctor who shared my mother's initial view that I was having a "temper tantrum" and *not* a seizure.

My parents weren't the kind of people to question authority. In their eyes, authority was smarter than they were. Intuition was a risk assessment based in ego rather than a divinely driven motive to be on the right path. Everyone else's intuition was right and theirs was obsolete if it didn't concur. There *was* a remedy and it was always *outside of ourselves.*

Not one day of my life had I considered the extent of growth, rejuvenation, and support my body had provided me with. Not one day did I consider that it was my friend. Quite the contrary. I felt victimized by it. I felt like it was a target the world shot at to point out my inferiority, powerlessness and temporary condition. My body was a pawn in the play of the world.

As many questions as I asked and as much as I honored the new information I was receiving about living a natural life, I still wasn't convinced that "I" was someone who could live that way.

My C-section was scheduled over my winter break at the community college I was attending. Attending a new school as a teenage pregnant person went exactly like this. I had one friend. I forget his name. He called me "P" for pregnant. He drew hysterical pictures of me as a stick figure having fifteen kids by the age of thirty. Having someone make fun of me in good heart was the lightest experience I'd had throughout a pregnancy I was supposed to keep hidden so I didn't gain eye traction toward my "mistake."

My decision to come alive, to choose life (my own and my unborn child's), to rebirth myself had me pretty damn driven. I was driven to get out. Out of my relationship when I could, out of my parent's home, out of school, out of hell. I had no idea what I wanted to get *into*, but I knew what I wanted out of. Until that time, I had honestly never thought about what I wanted a day in my life.

Every time I said I wanted anything, what I received was a lecture about how I should be grateful. "Want, want, want! All you do is want!" I'd hear. Those words changed my relationship with desire. At a very young age, I shifted from desiring possibility, to thinking of what I wanted only in terms of hoping more of what I didn't want, didn't show up.

That's how everyone around me thought. Always and in all ways, wait for the other shoe to drop and observe keenly where it will land when it does.

I'd reached a point that I'd perceived every shoe I'd ever thought to think of falling on my head, did, multiple times, leaving me dazed and confused living inside of a body with a face I didn't know. A beach plane flying a banner along the coast came into my mind's eye, waving a sign that read, "Fuck the shoes. Let em fall. Dodge them when you can, but don't let rubber soles, stop you from leaping forward with your own soul." They fell. They fucked me all up and somehow I was still standing.

One day in the middle of a parking lot, I stopped dead in my tracks, opened my arms and heart wide to the sky and said, "I know you're doing something good for me universe. To you, I say, bring it bitch! I'm in! Show me what you've got!" *(with reverence of course).*

What I did know now, I was driven to come alive. To me, that looked like challenging myself in healthy ways as much as possible. Every other challenge previous to now was some masochistic play with God as to how much suffering I could endure. This challenge was an obstacle course on the road to receiving bliss over suffering.

Beginning a full, new semester two weeks after I stepped into motherhood felt healthy somehow. So, that was the plan.

I was raised on chicken patties, mac and cheese, peanut butter and jelly, and icing. Another healthy challenge was incorporating raw foods into my diet. Eating anything to avoid earth's real food, I ate containers of store bought cake icing as meals my entire life. Set aside the fact that I was working with a conscious group of energy workers by accident at the time, they were also raw food advocates which I thought was very odd. One of the woman with skin that looked better than a porcelain doll ate raw ostrich! They were weird in a way I hadn't come to know weird. But, further than my intrigue of their weirdness, they were intelligent and articulate and I wanted to be intelligent and articulate.

My intelligence in high school was summed up like this: My humanities teacher spotted me half asleep drawing on my desk. Apparently he had asked a question directed at me which I didn't respond to. His class was right after my internship at the nature center. Likely, I didn't respond because I was stoned from my drive back. Rather than ask again, he picked up a chalkboard eraser and threw it at the wall right in front of my nose. The dust showered me. When I looked up in shock, he screamed, "Stacy Hoch! You are one of the smartest damn people that ever walked through this door and you just don't give a shit! God Damn it!" And, that was it. I never answered his question.

Three years later, here I was, having a kid, working, going to school, and had gotten through getting my vagina de-vag-ed by a laser, addictions, bulimia and all the other bull shit. I wanted to know the *me* my humanities teacher saw. I sure as hell never saw her. I was so consumed in avoiding being seen, in avoiding going home, in avoiding what hurt, I never made time to see myself, behind the veil I'd diligently crafted for myself to hide behind. I thought the veil was me, but my teacher saw through it.

By night, I laid my hands with reiki energy over my bulging, moving from the inside, belly. By day, I forced myself to eat a few fruits or vegetables, and I embarked on the journey of intelligent articulation.

I sat in a dark hallway with disgustingly stupid carpeting, waiting for my parents to exit my classroom from their parent-teacher conference in second grade. My mom came out crying and pushed my shoulder to get me out of the chair, indicating that I should move my ass. She was pissed. She was embarrassed. She was offended.

"*They said you'll never be a straight A student.*"

"So?" My six year old self was confused.

"They said you'll never be as smart as the other kids."

Oh. I got it loud and clear. My mother cared deeply about keeping up with the Jones'. While saying she wanted me to fit in, she also wanted me to stand out, but in all of the *right* ways.

She'd scold me or hit me over academics. She'd scream and yell, and confuse me like crazy. Then, she'd read what I was supposed to read, or do the homework I was supposed to do because I was, "too stupid to do it." I was confused and my self-esteem about taking initiative of anything at all was non-existent.

If I didn't try, I couldn't fail. But, I was already failing. And, when I did try, I got yelled at for not succeeding the first time. Academically and domestically, I was paralyzed.

By fourth grade, I sat at a table of four as the center of ridicule for being "fat and stupid." I cried every day when I got home from school, but this was nothing new.

In first grade, my teacher was one of those teachers who'd slam her big stick on desks and belittle her students into listening. I was sensitive so when she'd yell, I'd cry because I didn't understand why she was yelling. Then, she'd scream at me for crying even if I wasn't the initial target of her discipline.

Every single morning my entire first grade year, I threw up. Hear me again. Every Single. Morning. My. Entire. First. Grade. Year. I. Threw. Up. and a majority of those mornings I had diarrhea. A few kids were removed from this old woman's class that year. I begged my mom to get me a new teacher. Rather than get me a new teacher, she took me to the doctor to find out what was wrong with me. When the doctor said *stress* was the problem, I received a lecture that went like this: "One day, you're going to have a boss that you hate and that hates you! So, you better just get damn well used to it now!"

If I can say anything about intelligence and articulation, it's that I was not given a moment to relax long enough to actually learn anything of value. I literally learned nothing academically in my formative years, but by the time I knew I could, I was so hidden within myself I wouldn't have even known where to begin learning. I wanted to learn what I wanted to learn, not what the world wanted to teach me because nothing good ever came from what the world had taught.

The people I was working with were patient, and weren't teaching me with reprimand. They were only sharing themselves, who they were and how they lived. I'd never connected with an adult that knew themselves, felt free to have fun, and share themselves kindly. I wanted to be free like them when I grew up.

I felt the closest thing to the kind of connection I wanted not by being in connection, but by observing it. Eight years old, staring at a family of five come happily together in hugs when the three kids' parents picked them up from camp, time moved in slow motion. I was so intrigued, I found myself in my first accidental moment of experiencing an alignment I wanted, rather than running away from things I hated. I wanted to know what they had. Mysterious to me, they seemed just as connected to their inner worlds in ways of confidence and power, as they seemed connected to each other.

My world stopped, except for them.

When the bubble of my intent focus popped, I was the only other person left in the field with no sense of direction as to how to get to my own mother. I wandered in the woods a bit that day until an adult found me to send me on my way, all because I was stunned motionless, by being witness to the kind of connection I'd always wondered about.

I wanted my baby to feel safe with me, to look at me, to share with me, and feel free with me, the way I'd felt while watching them. The time to grow up and be in the 'real world", whether I asked for it or not, was now.

They always warned me about the "real world," instilling "grow up" principles since I could formulate a thought. Who "they" are, which is the "they" we all talk about when we say "they say...," I'll never know with the exception of my parents. I've come to know what "they" say, doesn't matter.

I needed to create a way to make growing up, feel like growing home. And growing home, had to feel like an open field on a warm, breezy day, and not like wilting to hell like the *real world* they threatened me with.

For now, cancer was on the back burner, my crater wounds were healed, and regardless of my past and present, my future became my only concern. Determined to leave a legacy beyond the shit I had swam in, in my thoughts and in my life, I had, for the first time, become a future-oriented woman-child, pregnant with her present legacy.

Making time to ruminate on the past, abuse, boyfriends, high school dramas, insecurities, was for the first time, not anywhere on my agenda. Carrying the past in all of my interactions, was too heavy a weight. I was gaining small tastes of the freedom that the people, who showed up as co-workers, but ultimately became my much needed mentors, were expressing. Freedom tastes like the wind and I wanted to live a life on the wings of it. Future focused to freedom is what I became.

I had no idea what was to come, but I was certain I'd make it better than the cesspool I knew. Well, that was my intent anyway.

Two Births In Less Than Two Years And About A Million Tiny Ones A Day.

"You must have chaos within you to give birth to a dancing star."

—*Friedrich Nietzsche*

I MET HIM! I finally got to meet Averiel! Well, I created him. Well, God created him. Whatever. You get it.

I was a nineteen year old girl who had never touched a newborn. I had no idea what motherhood was going to be like, but I was determined to do it with a mother's grace I'd never known.

Their needles scared me. According to the nurses, it's always the people with the most tattoos that complain about their fear of needles. I shivered, strapped to a bed as they sliced open my guts and pulled my baby boy from the only home he'd ever known into bright florescent lights with men in masks and big hands forcefully handling his little body. My boyfriend sat next to my face as I puked in a bucket, while they stitched me up and briefly showed me my son.

It's almost confusing to see your first child for the first time. Especially under circumstances that require boundaries and face masks with strangers who are in charge of the both of you. The moment I saw him, he was merely the outcome of this process, still unknown to me, his own person that I was now to care for. He was not mine *(because nothing that was mine ever stayed)*, but I, was his.

When they wheeled me back into my room, my mother had unexpectedly made herself a seat next to the window with tears in her eyes. He was the boy she'd always wanted, certainly, but her tears felt more meaningful than her typical "you're ruining your life if you keep this kid" stance, or the fact that he was a boy. She stopped herself from being seen in tears and said, "I saw him." That was pretty much the only thing she said to me during my hospital stay.

The nurses raved about him being the most beautiful boy they had ever seen, and they all assured me that they didn't say that to make mothers feel good. They meant it. I believed them.

I'd always felt disgusted by pictures of newborns. They looked like scrunched up aliens which was cute in its vulnerability, but definitely not cute as far as *attractive* was concerned in my book. But he was different. He looked like a newborn baby with a sweet toddler face.

Laid up in bed, healing from a body newly sliced apart to remove the largest growth it had known, I held my baby. Staring into his eyes, tears flooding from my own for three hours straight during the most ecstatic high I'd known. I *swore* I'd never get high again. I swore it to myself and I swore it to every person around, but I was swearing on most high to the majestic miracle of my son's life. His presence didn't bring an escapism high. It brought a transcendent high that the raw foodists and reiki practitioners would've understood.

New Year's Eve rolled around during my hospital stay which was a frantically avoidant experience on behalf of my boyfriend. His presence at the hospital was marked with nervous cleaning, and creating odd, unnecessary jobs for himself to distract himself from engaging in our very fresh reality. He told me his friends were having a NYE party and asked if it'd be cool if he went out. I stared at him from twenty feet behind my eyes and knew this was exactly what our relationship was going to be like. He didn't go at my sensitive request. Instead, he stayed, resentfully with *nothing to do.*

Breastfeeding wasn't coming easy and the nurses convinced me that my baby was in danger because he had lost one too many ounces for their liking. They gave him formula against my request although I had plenty of milk from using the breast pump. When I caused enough of a ruckus, they began using my milk, pouring it from a tiny syringe and taping the end of a small tube to my nipple for the baby to suckle out of. Except, milk flow wasn't the problem. The way he was latching onto the breast was.

I went home determined to make it work despite discouraging words from my family about not being a cow, that it was disgusting to feed a child that way, and that I needed to cover up because I was constantly exposed while trying to make the process a success.

January 1st, I stepped into independent motherhood. Averiel, wrapped up in a polar bear suit, on the brightest day of winter that year, sat next to me in the middle seat while I sat in the right window seat in the back of my boyfriend's car. Every car, railing, tree that came semi-close to us made my whole being react in resistance to this precious cargo being taken from me. I was now the protector of a life.

I'd never looked at my own life as valuable of protecting, and this was my first taste of loyalty to the sanctity of life on this plane. In honoring him, *life* itself was being honored, rather than honoring the dark places of doom my mind was typically worshipping.

I woke up on my parents couch from my first nap in motherhood, startled because I'd accidentally fallen asleep and wasn't sure if he was still alive. The kind of moment every first time mom goes through when we stick our fingers under our baby's nose to make sure they're still breathing.

A few days later, my boyfriend had people over to party. I locked myself and my baby in the bathroom of my parents' home and sobbing, I promised him I wouldn't let the stupidity of people who didn't understand the magnitude of his presence interfere with his perfect right to be perfectly cared for. That day I knew, I was destined for single parenthood sooner than later. At the time, call me selfish or naive, or both, I'd rather have had him not have a father than have two parents that hated each other.

I was reminded frequently throughout my life that the day I was born is the day my parent's relationship ended. My mother devoted herself to me and lost interest in my father. My mother cried in her room for three weeks before returning to work, staring at my father from the same windows I was now looking down at my boyfriend partying with his friends through, as my father and his friends snorted coke while my mother *selflessly devoted* herself to the life of a kid she didn't want. In her eyes, my father got away with murder. Hers. Her life was now over because of me, and he never took the time to acknowledge her. So, she resented us both.

I didn't want to share these stories with my son. I wanted him to feel chosen. I wanted him to know he belonged and that I didn't sacrifice my life for him, but I invested my everything for the benefit of *our* life. I saw a much easier means of providing him with the love I wanted him to experience without his father absent-mindedly showing up. I didn't perceive he'd be capable of the kind of love I wanted my son to know.

If it's any consolation to understanding the dynamic of my son's parents as a couple, a group of friends we both shared in my first semester of college nicknamed us as a duo: "ghetto hippie." He wore leather jackets, carried guns, and dreamed of muscle cars and mansions. He was also on the run from the repo guys and as I said, my weed dealer when we met.

A friend's band advertised with posters that read: "Come see Shady Nook -and Stacy, the Dancing Hippie." That was me, Stacy the Dancing Hippie. In psychological terms, I was Jung: cosmic, soft, introspective and collective. I saw thousands of potential viewpoints where other people saw two. He was Jay Haley, a family therapist that didn't care about the root of the problem, only that the *consequence* of *having* the problem be enough to stop the problem. I lived in another world attempting to get my feet on the ground *in this one* and he lived steadfastly on an earth of materialism and pursuit.

Though I wanted him to succeed and I loved him as a person, I knew what everyone that saw us from the outside knew. We were both compromising our individual integrities by staying together.

He supported me though. He trusted my decisions and though he made none of his own, he gave me the reigns on parenting. Some may say it was his cop out, but I needed him to hand me self-trust in this regard. I spent my whole life fighting the world on everything and this one little tiny baby that was my own, he freed me not to have to fight for *(in the beginning anyway)*.

I still had to put up a good fight to my parents, to the doctors that wanted to inject my baby with things I didn't agree with, who condescendingly advised my naivety. Most of all though, I had to put up a good fight with my own self-doubt. Breastfeeding was a disaster. I resigned sorrowfully to the breast pump within a week. I was determined to give him nutrients that'd best serve him even if he wouldn't suckle it from my breast.

I went to school by night when my parents were home to watch him, and pumped breastmilk every three hours for the first seven months of his life. I set alarms to wake up even when he was asleep just to keep an ample milk supply.

I had a cryosurgery for cervical dysplasia *(pre-cancer cells)* when he was five months old that couldn't be done when I was pregnant.

The atmosphere was grim and I was determined to know better. I was learning so much about family patterns, epigenetics, the transmission of traumas through DNA, healing on cellular levels, and myself.

I wanted to bring my son up with a virgin gut (by only and exclusively giving him breastmilk for the first entire year of his life), but I had to leave him with people who undermined every authentic decision I made.

"Oh, it's not going to kill him!"

"You're depriving the child! It's so-and-so's birthday. Let him eat cake."

I was also confident in my decision to have extremely limited screen time. My investment was in choosing wisely and consciously rather than blindly making choices based on tradition. I researched day and night. Vaccines. Chemicals. Electromagnetic pollution. Veganism. Natural healing. Plants as medicine. Spiritual ceremony for integrated healing.

Every one of these topics and more consumed me with a sense of both power and helplessness.

I'd made the closest decision I could on vaccinations at the time to mend the bridge between what I believe and what the world shoved down my throat. I decided to do an extended schedule of when he would receive his shots. Though it wasn't completely the decision I wanted to be making, I felt it was my safest bet to not looking like a naive nineteen year old know-it-all twit. It felt powerful to claim a stance on what felt like a common bridge. But, my doctors didn't like me questioning the other side of the bridge I believed we were building, toward a middle ground, and they definitely didn't hesitate to let me know.

He was sick once. I was driving home from school and had an intuitive nudge when I couldn't get a hold of my mother that she'd made him a doctor's appointment against my judgement. I trusted the order of his body to heal itself without antibiotics. Where I saw viruses and decided to wait it out, my mother saw her daughter being willful and neglectful. I called the doctor to see if she had made an appointment. She had. It was *over the top*, threatening, because she'd been swearing she was going to take him to get all of his vaccines despite my attempts to educate her about why I was making the decision I was. What I did know for sure, was, you don't give a sick kid a vaccine. You just don't. Convenience or not, you just don't.

The appointment she had made was scheduled for five minutes from the moment I made the call. I was ten minutes away. I sped there, walked in and let the nurses know that my son was in an appointment. I needed to be let in.

They weren't getting it, so I opened the door to the hallway where the patient rooms were. The assistants quickly pushed me back behind the door to gather information about why I was there. They eventually led me to the room where my mother and son were. Upon my arrival, my mother and I shook our heads *"no"* at each other, while we stared each other down. We both knew what we were doing. The doctor agreed with me. It's a virus, it will pass, keep him comfortable. Then my mother began a rant about demanding the doctor explain the risks of an extended vaccination schedule.

I had researched so much, traditional doctors, *especially condescending ones*, were the last people I'd listen to about real healing. I didn't need her to tell me a thing. But, she began. I responded defensively. I wasn't going to change my mind. Here I was, being the nineteen year old, naive in their eyes, know it all twit, and though I held my ground, a feeling of constant defeat never left. Every corner I turned, my mother was standing there as an image that haunted any speckle of trust I had in myself, turning it to a paralyzing stone of self-doubt and shame. When the doctor asked me if I was going to provide my son with the vaccination he'd be due for that day, I said *no*. The doctor snapped, "Then why do you bring him here?" and I snapped back, "I didn't! My mother did!"

I cried the entire way home. Confused and unsupported as ever. Support, cannot be understated. It is life-blood and soul food. In its absence, the devil steps in to dance.

Some will say, I was being willful, or ungrateful. After all, as my parents always had, they provided for my physical needs in the sense that they gave me food and a roof, but gave me no legs to stand on in my own life.

My mother's unrealized dream was to own a bakery. She'd bake a whole batch of brownies and I'd eat half. I didn't want to, *damn it!* I was addicted to food and I knew better. She didn't eat them. When she ridiculed me for being a *hog*, I asked her to give them away, or better yet, not make them. Her response was, "Just don't eat them! I don't!"

When I asked who she was making them for she'd say, *herself.*

I was trying desperately to grab any thread of life that looked promising and every thread I grabbed, I felt was delicately and deliberately cut by my mother with a smiling Betty Crocker-like face.

Indeed, I was grateful we had a room to sleep in. Indeed, I was grateful that in an emergency, my parents would show up. Indeed, I was grateful they took an interest in my son though they pulled him in every direction that looked like it was away from mine.

I just wanted some say in my life and still, every peep of a rational voice I made for myself was drown out by blow-horn-like denounces of my validity.

Being constantly sick didn't help. My childhood was infested with over pre-scribed antibiotics and I'd only known to attack my body for not doing its job. I'd never considered that my body was communicating with me through its ill-nesses, but now, I knew it was saying something, I just couldn't pinpoint what.

By the time Averiel was a year old, I'd dove deeply into hormonal effects on mood and body rhythms and decided to completely irradiate birth control from my body. My mother wanted me on birth control when she smelled a scent of possibility that I'd be having sex after I first got my period. So, at thirteen, my sister drove me to the clinic and I came home with a child's mind, in a teenagers body, with a bag of adult contraception. On and off for years, birth control was a staple in my body, strangle-holding my cells. Ironically, like my conception being a hit or miss phenomenon during my mother's eight days free of an IUD stint, I was wearing the patch when I got pregnant with Averiel, but it fell off like a Band-Aid in water.

I felt an intuitive nudge that another baby wanted to come through. And secretly, I really wanted that to be true.

It makes no sense, right? Except, I was raised as an only child, though I had four older sisters. The youngest of them was ten years older than I was. By and large, I was alone, and the world reiterated to me that I was an only child. I grew into the role of buffer for my parents, always wishing for the kind of shared history my sisters lives created together. The lens I saw life through was insane and all I ever wanted was someone to bear witness through my telescope to bounce back some light that assured me they saw it too.

My parents couldn't stand each other, I presented a problem. My parents couldn't pay the bills, I distracted them with a depression. My parents didn't want to face an issue or each other, they faced me and any imaginary issue they wished I'd had, so they didn't have to heal themselves. I was also their trusty secret keeper which never panned out well.

After two years of carrying the weight of my father's affair, I stayed home from school in a depressed stare. My mother felt the weight of how big this depression was as I'd been so physically ill and emotionally lifeless, I'd missed a majority of school my freshman year of high school.

For whatever reason, she stayed home with me that day and sat beside me on the couch, berating me for not having *any reason* to be depressed. I reluctantly opened into a conversation with tears running down my face, knowing that not for her, but for me, I had to tell her what weight I was carrying. The lie I'd been living. I cried not for her, but for my father, the man I was about to betray by baring *his* soul to my mother. When I told her *(only the half of it)* she threw up her hands, "Oh my God! That's what you're depressed about?! Everyone has one night stands Stacy!" and she somewhat blew it off letting me know she'd known he had cheated on her before.

Ok, so was I crazy or was she crazy? I thought I was carrying this weight to protect her from her wounds and to protect my father from his affairs, but here she was telling me I was an idiot for being concerned about something I believed was important to her.

I liked being the bearer of secrets to a degree because it made me feel like I belonged. Keeping secrets, in ways, was my leverage and my worth. Deep down, I knew it was a superficial tactic that was more dangerous than helpful. With each secret they both shared with me, I made up stories between every word they chose to share or not to share about it. I was certain my mother would be devastated and I wanted to protect her from her devastation. I remained devastated in doing so. Telling her, didn't devastate her! I realized I was devastated because I had *made up a story* that she *would* be. Two years of my life, I carried that big secret but that secret I believed was big, ended up resulting in this and only this: "Eli! It's pretty sad that your fifteen year old daughter has to tell me you're having an affair." The end. And, life as we knew it, continued.

What a confusing mess for my psyche.

They projected onto me what they wanted to see, to keep themselves safe from having to look inside of themselves. With all of the tension in the house between me and my parents, I knew my son, was accidentally and unconsciously taking over my role of buffer. I knew he was now the one being pulled between them and I'd subconsciously felt relieved by his presence in my old role. I'd come to an awareness that much like I'd felt my mother offered me to the world as a sacrificial lamb, I was doing the same to my son on a *(questionably)* smaller alter.

If this was so, I didn't want him to be alone. I wanted him to have a partner so there was less potential for a triangle effect where his sweet little soul was pulled by two opposing forces. If he had a sibling, they'd be the base and anyone else would be the one who was pulled, not them. I didn't see a way out of the situation anytime soon, so my subconscious notion was to add to it. Breathe a bit more life into it. Literally.

Maybe they'd force me out on my own and it'd finally be *the out* I was looking for. None of this was conscious to me at the time of course. Real as ever, though.

Every time I spoke of moving out on my own, I heard things like, "You don't even give this child a bath every day! He'll never get a bath if you're on your own." Or, "You'll never be able to feed him. What would you do if it wasn't for us?" Mind you, I don't agree with giving babies a daily bath, nor did I feed him anything but breastmilk until he was a year old, but for years, I questioned whether my decisions were made out of genuine intuition or pure rebellion of my mother's way of life. Every projected doubt played me into a submissive, stoned rebel who was screaming to be heard in my truth, but acting only in my fear.

What we see, we practice, and what we practice, we master. Just like my parents, my daily practice had led me to repeating the practice of stuck-ness, rather than opening to a practice that stimulated progress.

It always came down to money. My mother always threatened that if I ever moved out, I'd be completely on my own. I'd never be allowed back and they wouldn't help me once I left. Seeing this dependency made me terrified that if I didn't leave them now, I'd become comfortable in our destructive patterns. I'd break down any ounce of courage I'd felt to break free from the mental concentration camps we mazed through on a daily basis.

My boyfriend and I rarely got along. My patterns with intimacy were hot and cold, very black and white, just as my mother's threats of disowning any amount of support she currently provided if I moved out. He'd do his best to stick up for my beliefs when my parents undermined my motherhood, but he was gone more than he was around, much like my own father. He had gotten a night job and began going to grad school.

We rarely had sex which was awesome for me because sex terrified me. STD's, pregnancies, cancer, vulnerability, all in a space that's supposed to be sacred. Every time I touched skin, I was slimed with a vibe of disgust. Certainly, I never wanted to be near a penis. After years of being a subject to a man's imagination and condescendingly hearing, "Suck my dick!" the thought of doing so was associated with a lack of choice. A forceful, disgusting surrender to being the subjectivity I resisted becoming.

We stayed together based on accumulation. We'd make plans and talk ourselves into them. Buy a dog. Now we're tied for a few years. Have a kid. Now we're tied for a lot more than a few years. Plan to move out. Now we have to face each other. We knew we wouldn't last once we did, which echoed a very familiar story, as most generationally charged inheritance does. But I wouldn't let my kids take the blunt of that reality. The part of an inheritance I got from a lineage of disconnection from self and the truth, was sure to stop with me. Of this, I swore.

The only time we had sex in three months, we got pregnant. I was twenty years old. I'm not sure if I subconsciously thought that my son's life was so motivating to my success that having another baby would set me on fire to take charge of my life, but I knew I felt another baby wanting to come and I didn't care to resist its desire to enter life, earth side.

When I got the news though, my best friend sat in the bathroom with me while Averiel climbed all over me as I sobbed uncontrollably on the floor. "What am I going to do???" with a quivering lip, is all I could muster up.

I'm pro-choice, but the fact that I already had a baby to show me what I'd be losing if I opted for abortion made the idea of abortion now obsolete. I couldn't. Well, I wouldn't *(at the time)*.

I called my boyfriend at work, hysterical and incomprehensible. When he finally got my message through my muffled cries, he said, "What about the morning after pill?"

I screamed, "It's not the morning after you fucking idiot!" and slammed the phone back onto its spot on the wall, sliding my back to the ground. I hated him. I knew I was in it alone. At least, I thought I was. Or better yet, maybe I wanted to be, but didn't want to admit it to myself.

We began looking at apartments before we told my parents. We tried to take a pro-active approach, but we both knew if we moved into what we could afford, we'd both be settling into a life we'd both want out of more than we wanted out of the one we had.

I shockingly don't remember much about my parents reaction to my second pregnancy which is odd because pretty much every day since I was fourteen my mother swore up and down I'd get knocked up as a teenager. She was always waiting for me to prove her right about what a fuck up I was. Now was her chance.

One kid, school by weekday, work all weekend, and a baby on the way, I was twenty years old and completely clean for the first time since I was twelve. No alcohol, no drugs, not even pot, which, mind you, I do believe was my medicine. Between the time I began smoking pot and I was eighteen years old, I only had one seizure. I went from having pretty regular seizures *though they did decrease in frequency the older I got*, to once in a decade with the introduction of recreational marijuana into my teenage-hood.

Even in my youngest years, like my conditioning for mental escapism, my seizures may have been my body's unconscious art of controlling the exit I was looking for, even if only for a moment of freedom in the blackness. Marijuana was hands down, my first dose of *real* medicine.

But now I was clean. Again, I opened up the conversation of natural childbirth, but my doctors said my pregnancies were too close in time to try a vaginal birth after caesarian due to a higher risk of placental rupture, which is potentially lethal.

My second pregnancy was harder than my first. The nausea was worse. I got much bigger, much quicker. I was still independent and happy enough to be asked out on dates by my college peers even though I was pregnant, with a kid, and a boyfriend. I mean, strokes to the ego when you're down are nice however superficial we know they are.

Expanding thoughts about how stuck in this situation I really was and how much of it I was choosing to stay stuck in, were reoccurring questions.

The mother-daughter relationship hadn't been something I'd experienced as sacred for myself in the role of a daughter. Finding out I was having a girl fueled my passion to know the sacredness of it, in any role I could. It was looking like if I was ever going to know what I'd longed to be given, it was about to be shown to me, by my *own* giving. I was about to become the mother of a daughter.

Averiel was ten days away from his second birthday when my daughter was born via caesarian section, again over my Christmas break during my junior year of college.

Aura Brijae came into the world, smaller and different looking than her perfectly shaped, sweet toddler faced brother. She was her own. The very first sentence out of my mouth when I saw her was a comparison. "Hi sweetheart!" I said. "Wow. You don't look anything like your brother." By nature, my family would prize a boy over a girl any day and by nurture, I would do everything in my power to protect her from the emotional realities they would place upon her for being born with a vagina. Yet, here I was, twenty one and stuck in the comparisons I wanted to protect her from.

My sweet curly haired almost two year old was still in diapers when my mom brought him to meet his baby sister. My baby girl and I laid chest to chest in a dark room, just the two of us. When Averiel walked in, in his two year old way, it reminded me of when I took him home from the hospital.

My first baby was my Siberian Husky, River. I was very adamant about having the dog and my new baby meet in a neutral place. I'd loved that dog so much I didn't even go straight home from the hospital when Averiel was born. We met at my grandparents' house for their introduction. River hadn't seen me in days. Naturally, her reaction was excited. She jumped up and nudged my brand new son's fragile head. I told myself I had to disconnect from her.

It was looking like I had to make a choice between my dog baby and my natural born baby. With the emotional resources I'd had at the time, it was all I could do to tend to my son and keep River, who was posing as playfully threatening, away from us. That's what I did. Averiel was born and my relationship with River took a back seat. Much like when I was born, my parents' relationship took a back seat.

I faced this same feeling again when my son *(who was huge for his age, by the way)* ran in like a bull in a china shop to meet his new baby sister. There I laid, wanting to protect her from the very thing I spent my last three years vowing to protect and the thought that I may disconnect from him to keep her safe was agonizing.

She also took right to nursing which naturally presented a more bonding experience than his birth for the both of us, despite the C-section and her stay in the NICU for supposedly low (I believe unfounded) oxygen levels.

Pregnancy hormones make *everything* feel exaggerated. I left the hospital in worse physical shape than my first C-section, and having serious doubts about whether I could love two children, undivided.

Love in my family was always based on a division. Always. In order to obtain love, I had to divide. In order to give love, I had to divide. Shame was a sick pleasure that my family spread around about as passive aggressively as blowing the seeds of a dandelion on a summer afternoon. Not particularly passive, not particularly aggressive, but somehow obvious when the breeze hits you in the face.

Truthfully in those first moments of parenting two babies, I wanted my son to feel guilty that he was still in diapers. I wanted him to know he wasn't everything anymore and in my own longings for pity, I guess I was secretly being reminded that I never got to be everything to anyone the way he did for the while I'd made him the center of the universe. Now his turn was up.

Pity was always my go-to. The only time I ever got attention that wasn't hurtful was when I was being hurt by something or someone else that was out of the control of my mother. I broke my arm, had a seizure, got sick, got depressed, you know how the rest goes. Mom paid attention without pouring salt on the wound when the world told me I was no one special and the wound wasn't inflicted by her.

These wounds, she got to be a different kind of savior for.

I learned pity very young and as a mother of two at twenty one, working my ass off simply to get out of the intensity of the life I had created for myself, I could've used some serious fucking pity.

Pity for myself and my babies, consumed me until the first time I was left alone with both of them. I slowly began to witness the process of true love that wasn't divided. This was an observation that didn't fall easy on my heart. In my own dedication to mindfully raise my children, every pound of anger I felt for not being tenderly cared for in all the ways I wanted for myself as a child, I filtered into mothering the little girl in me, by mothering them.

They didn't hurt me when I hugged them. They didn't reject me when I told them I loved them. They let me be me, and I, them. Still, I didn't know where their father fit. I was learning the lesson of love undivided, but defensively believed in order to continue this undivided love I was cherishing, I had to protect it, by keeping him out when he didn't show up like I believed someone who was loving, should. Just like the dog, and much like my initial fears of having to protect one child over another.

I never knew whole love, but in my attempts to know it, I ostracized anything that I believed interfered with the kind of love I wanted my children to have, including their father. Mind you, this was subconscious ostracizing and quite frankly, I don't think he cared, because it let him off the hook of every responsibility of connection he may have had to feel. Had I not let him skirt out of the vulnerable role of fatherhood by being "enough" for him, playing both masculine and feminine, my children would likely only have a mother today, and not a father. If I revealed to him what it's like when shit actually gets real in parenthood, he would've left.

It got quiet for a bit in my relationship with him likely because he always wanted a girl. Her birth somehow motivated him differently. Considerably, too much. He worked all day which kept us distant and distracted from having to face each other, but afforded us a house of our own. He also didn't need to work the way he was. We were basically kids and he was close to finishing his Master's Degree and making six digits.

He wasn't present. He made a lot of money and blew a lot of money. We had to dig for change in the kids piggy banks multiple times. I made every single decision ever made about the kids. He trusted me which is honorable, but in his trust, he left me. Almost as if he believed in me so much, that I didn't need him, and in turn, to him, it seemed as if the kids had both of their parents. Me!

What I haven't shared is the multiple times he left me, for other woman, for drugs, or me kicking him out during my borderline romantic pendulum swings. That was a big thing for us. He spent money on pot, which though I didn't smoke, I would've been fine with, had we had the money to pay our bills. Our arguments and disconnections always rode on the surface of different-in-kind, but equal in *intensity*, callousness.

Motherhood changes you. Parenthood changes you. It just does. I published an article once about motherhood and a woman came at me saying that a mother should not get to know herself through her children, but that she should *already* know herself. My entire life I wished my mother would have just found herself. My mother has always "known" herself, and she prided herself in that fact. I, however, believed my mother was hidden somewhere inside of herself surrounded by her own guilt and shame, exactly where she'd taught me to stay. If for one day my mother would have been open to change, my life would have been drastically different.

She gave up her life for me in her eyes. I swore to myself to *begin* my life for my children, *never to give it up*. Motherhood is built on changing us. I let it change me under the condition that my relationship to motherhood will change me into more of *who I already am* on the inside despite what the world wants me or my motherhood to look like.

The most natural way to describe this process is in the art of getting to know more of yourself daily, by way of love. Children are an incredible gift offered to us in the process of creating who we wish we'd had in our own times of uncertainty. That's what I vowed to do for my children. Be the mother I cried and longed for countless times. My cries were met in the womb of my invisible friends.

As I mothered my own soul, as I became as gentle on myself as I was with my children, I was shaping out who I wanted to become without the constant pressure of who I *had* to be in order to survive. Shapeshifting now to meet myself, rather than the expectations of acquiescing for the world.

Their father was never around, so exploring myself through meditation, yoga, art, and parenting, was the quietest my life had ever been. I stayed with him because he offered me the opportunity to be at peace for twelve hours of what could've posed to be very long and lonely mothering days. I filled that time with soul searching and research, finding natural doctors, and nutritionists.

I believed one day one of us would finally leave. I didn't want to be the used goods, herpes and HPV infested, insecure, hot and cold, single mom with two kids, and twenty some years of baggage trailing behind me when it ended.

Graduating in the top of my class at Penn State, I walked down the aisle after we listened to the Freedom Writers author give her speech. As my left hand swung forward *as it does when we walk*, my sweet, curly blond haired almost three year old, popped out from the chairs and grabbed my fingers. That was the moment I first believed a better life was actually ahead of us. I wasn't making it up in some Stacy escapism la-la land story. He walked the rest of the path with me while tears of relief poured down my face, to the rhythm of the audience cheering.

His hand in mine, was the first time I realized his growing hands would touch me doing every single thing I'd ever do, and I wanted him to be proud. His hands in mine were the first hands I ever touched that I believed were proud to hold mine. I'd never hurt him. I'd never let him down so long as I could help it and I'd do all that I could to ensure that he remained excited to celebrate life's moments with me. Obviously this notion transferred to my daughter as well, but it was in his act of connection being witnessed by others, that I believed my life, like I begged my mother to find within herself, was somewhere deep inside of me, worth living.

All of their father's actions led me to believe he was temporary, so I squeezed what I could for the sake of saying I tried until there was no juice left. Time proved there was still some juice. I did a lot of *his* graduate school homework, so I knew I could handle grad school. Three weeks after I graduated college, I had a full graduate school schedule. I was home by day and in school by night. In retrospect, signing up for graduate school right away was a socially acceptable mirror image of my own resistance to step into the *real world* I was still afraid of.

Aura suffered from colic. Well, we all suffered from her colic. I didn't sleep through a solid night until she was eighteen months old. I was pregnant with Averiel, nursed *(by pumping)* for almost a year, got pregnant with Aura very soon after I gave up breastfeeding, and then nursed her. Essentially, my body was operating on pregnancy and post-natal hormones for almost four years straight.

Months after her birth came agoraphobia.

Then, came the memories.

Unearthing Roots Of The Crazy Tree.

"The spiritual path wrecks the body and afterwards, restores it back to health. It destroys the house to unearth the treasure, and with that treasure builds it better than before."

—*Rumi*

CHEWING ON BITS of intellectual and spiritual freedom proved more fear provoking than I'd suspected. At first, it's like a walk through a flower field that we're sure is covertly a mine field, beautifully disguised.

Every thought I had was riddled with some predatory tragedy that I, or intruders, inflicted onto my children, or onto me. Namely, my daughter. There was something about giving birth to a daughter that triggered an avalanche of suffocating feelings I wouldn't wish upon an enemy. I was torn between the intensity of my thoughts and the dullness of my reality where my emotions were concerned. I began not to trust myself or anyone in a different way than my lack of trust before. While I felt an intense need to protect my children from the world, I felt a more intense need to protect them from *myself.* I couldn't understand the nature of my thoughts, but I was sure my dead grandmother, somehow, somewhere, could understand.

Here's the rabbit hole my train wreck thoughts might've went down in any given second: What if my daughter is molested by me?! What if I walk with a knife while I'm cooking and accidentally stab one of the kids when they are crawling? What if I fall down the steps carrying one of them? Why would I think about molesting my daughter? I'd never do it! Everyone hates me. They all think

I'm stupid. An inconvenience. I should just kill myself. I can't kill myself because I have kids. My kids may be better off without me.

Every fear I had, felt like a new version of an ancient feeling that lurked in my unconscious. Stories I'd put to rest had resurfaced from their graves. A perpetual feeling of being stuck in between someone telling me to *do* something, *me doing it*, and then being told I was *naughty for listening to them*, felt like a thunderstorm that followed me everywhere. The experience of not knowing what I was doing wrong and the consequences of what my actions and thoughts were capable of, hid in every corner in the maze of a mind I was once again, a prisoner of.

I wanted to puke it out, to revert to scratching my skin off, to binge eat it away. Mainly what I did was sit paralyzed in fear, searching my life for clues of how, who, and what, got me to this point. I needed someone to hold accountable for the mind fuck I'd found myself in. I was pretty certain it wasn't I who was responsible. Again, the invisible hand moving the pawn picked me up from my fake-it-till-you-make-it queen status, and moved me like the pawn I'd been, onto a square I was sure was murderous to my soul.

I dug for any clear imagery that made sense. A bitter feeling that it was right on the tip of my brain, knowing I could never actually get to it, was the only constant that surfaced.

When my mom did make me sleep in my own room on the nights my father was home, my room was the bridge to get to my sister's room. Whoever lived with us at the time in our half-way-house like atrium for social rejects, all of my sisters' friends, my friends, and all of my sisters' boyfriends had access to my room as a throughway to get upstairs. Thus, they had access to me.

Maybe my mom was covertly trying to protect me? I remembered glimpses of being uncomfortable when my sister's boyfriend crawled into bed with me. I remembered a babysitter threatening to tell my parents about our sexual anatomy class play because I told her I didn't want her to swim in my pool with her bully neighborhood friends and stuffing down the feeling of wanting to stab her in the throat because she was at the forefront of our explorations though she was older, *and* in charge of us.

Ruminating thoughts about what kind of a mother leaves her daughter with a known or at minimum, *accused* sexual abuser, pushing it under the rug for the benefit of not stirring things up in the unspoken-rules of the silence-department in the family enraged me. I couldn't put my finger on it, but I knew there was something my fingers remembered that my mind didn't.

Though I was sexually active, I'd never *had* sex with anyone. I *gave* sex to my partners. Penises terrified me as if they were something to give into and vaginas were dirty, yet here I was having extremely uncomfortable thoughts about what I might do with a vulnerable one.

This was old stuff. That much was obvious. Without a clear explanation for the subjects of my thoughts, my umbrella feeling was resentment for my own childhood. Realizing how incredibly unsafe I'd always felt, I wanted better for my kids. Wrapping my head around the idea that a mother, any mother could say or do the things mine did, or make choices about my life with the intent of remaining *cheap*, while looking rich, was a new task for me. I wasn't sure I wanted to understand, but I was sure that my own safety issues needed to be dealt with, so I didn't pass them down to my children through thought, or experience.

Until then, I hadn't once since childhood, looked at my lifelong feelings of displacement and mistrust as abnormal. I thought everyone ended up as jaded as I did growing up, hiding somewhere deep inside of themselves, afraid to come out. I also suspected this was the reason for the world being so fucked. If this perpetual feeling was normal, I felt like an incredibly selfish person for bringing children into the world to contend with for the unpredictable entirety of their lives. Wallowing, every single thing felt like a re-traumatization which felt like a neon sign flashing "You are in hell" on my forehead that blinded me from anything worth seeing. The hell I had spent my life rebelling against had planted its seeds in my cells and grew a fiery garden using my blood as soil. It wouldn't leave.

I came up with behaviors to make my way more subtly. I counted every single step on every single staircase, until I memorized the familiar staircases. I silently celebrated not killing my children when I touched the floor at the end of the stairs. I changed diapers, steering clear of cleaning out too much from my daughter's crevices because I didn't know what the intentions behind my fucked up thoughts were. I tucked all of the knives away into drawers and if I did have to use one, I held the handle so tightly I could've been likened to a professional football player who never drops the ball. I stayed away from mirrors. I took less baths because the most persistent visual I had related to a bath tub was of me, sliced wrists, bleeding out, in a pool of tragically beautiful blood that indicated I was caught in the surrendered moments between life and death. The moments I'd found to be so peaceful watching my grandmother die.

I couldn't leave the house. I tried. I had a degree in psychology and enough life wisdom to know this was a rabbit hole triggered by an onset of something that needed my attention and I needed to get through it quicker than later. Why those thoughts? Why these images? Countless times, I sat with my head between my knees, long hair touching the floor, limp necked squeezing my temples together with the insides of my knees, pleading for my mind to stop.

Then there was food. Once again, my focus on food, on body, on how disgusting any aspect of myself that reminded me of sexuality was. Though I was sustainably the thinnest for the longest I'd ever been *due to breastfeeding and a serious dietary lifestyle overhaul,* my obsessive thoughts took me out of every moment I'd otherwise be happily present to my children in.

I took the kids to the park and found myself distracted, thinking about donuts I hadn't eaten in years.

There's a very specific vibration that only those of us who have been back handedly forced to know, can attest to. It's similar to every time our family walks out of a buffet, lethargic and sloppy, complaining that they ate too much, and sloth like, we feel the empty fullness in our own guts, riddled with shame for over extending ourselves into…nothing. Somehow that's what the vibration feels like. Overly full, about to burst, emptiness tainted with a grime feeling, that *food* became the symbol of simultaneous resistance and desire for.

Food was my armor and my weapon against myself that from the inside looking out, felt like it controlled my thoughts. Not even my thoughts about *it*, but my thoughts about *me*! I'd look at pizza and think, "disgusting." I ate pizza and would think, "Disgusting." Therefore, most of what I ingested was swallowed with an assault against myself for *being* disgusting.

The big fuck you I used, to spitefully buck to the world as a building block of what the world saw of me, was being internalized. Every bite of food I took was chewed in the letters F-U-C-K Y-O-U and swallowed whole, leaving me fucked by a pimp I was codependent on, but hated. Dirty. You get the point, it was rough. So rough in fact, I forced my agoraphobic ass into church room circles holding hands with self-proclaimed food addicts in *overeaters anonymous.*

Like a still shot of a car accident right before impact in front of your face when you finally surrender to the reality that you're about to total your car and potentially never see your family again, I watched my destructive thoughts and feared the totality of the damage that they could do.

I saw his hand. In my mind, I saw that he was missing a finger.

His hand was on my right thigh, just below my shorts as I sat on his lap steering his black pickup truck because he asked me if I wanted to. I saw every image of sexual play I'd ever embarked on with the neighborhood girls. I was grasping strings at a space that felt like it was holding together the threads just on either side of victim or perpetrator and I couldn't figure out which one I was on. What stood out the most was the memory that had just surfaced for me about the time my mom punched me in the face for screaming "Rape!" at my grandfather's house. I considered that my mother was a molester. My teenage therapist thought that. Actually, she straight up said that to me followed by, and if not that, she has exceptionally poor boundaries.

Therapists were *crocks of shit* according to my family. Word on the street was that my aunt conjured up false memories because of her therapist. Maybe these feelings of panic weren't even my own. Maybe they were passed down through the unresolved conflicts my aunt faced, bleeding all over my moments. Imprinted like ghosts into my lineage, maybe they'd come into my current space time in order to resolve themselves through me. Whether they were mine or not, I hounded down the trail of their source for my daughter's sake.

I considered my babysitters merely let us run amuck and play sexual games we were told we should be ashamed of. I considered every story under the sun about why these thoughts and images were coming up for me, but I knew the fact that I had a girl, *and not a boy* was the finger that pulled the trigger.

His absent finger was never in the forefront of my mind. I knew him my entire life and completely forgot he didn't have a finger, but the memory was so clear. He sawed it off in a farming accident. It wasn't making sense. Neither was I. I didn't trust the world and I certainly didn't trust myself and that left my kids floating on cheap life boats out in the middle of an ocean storm with no calm in the forecast.

I dropped out of graduate school. I was voiceless, afraid, and on the verge of a psychosis I knew my family would want me to keep very quiet about.

I found a natural doctor who accepted my insurance. At a new patient consult, I told her my baby had colic and though there was nothing "wrong" with her by vision, she wasn't totally right. She acted like she was hurting all the time. I was the only one who was willing to hear her cries as a call for help, rather than an annoying baby who wants to be spoiled (which is what I was told). Despite the few times I had to leave her out of complete frustrated exhaustion, so I didn't get out of control angry, I wore her in an attachment style parenting method, in pretty much, every moment. Still, she needed more than Averiel did. Way more. The extent of her needs were over the top, even for an infant.

Red curly hair, thin, and apparently pissed off, the doctor stood up and threw her arms backwards and then up in the air and said, "STOP VACCINATING YOUR DAUGHTER!" Immediately, I blobbed into a sopping mess. She was listening! She gave me permission to validate my own desires for not relying on an industry I didn't buy into. She ranted, "They hyper stimulate your immune system, they contain mercury, and a live virus!...." that was the closest to lay man's terms that she made sense. She was yelling. Literally, yelling at me, the same way the other doctor yelled at me with an opposing message. I wanted her to keep yelling. I wanted to see how passionate she was about the passion I myself had, but felt I wasn't allowed to express. She was a doctor, overly educated, professional, a mother, and she didn't call me stupid or naive for questioning vaccines. She called me stupid for not trusting my own intuition.

I looked up at her, limp from weeping, hair in my face and said, "You're the first person that listened to me as a mother. I need you to listen to me as a woman. I need help. Serious help. I need you to listen and I don't want you to lock me away, and I'm intelligent and educated, and I know better than to actually follow through, but the thoughts I'm having, I'm not sure if it's because I'm sleep deprived and nursing, or if I just totally awoke to a repressed reality and now I fear that any and all of the things that've happened to me will happen to my own daughter, but I'm having horrible thoughts. *Like bad.* I can't leave the house. Everyone hates me according to me, and my scariest one is I am going to molest my daughter. I know I never would, but the thought scares me. I can't stop them. I think I need to be medicated."

She smiled at me, told me I should eat some red meat once a week to regulate my blood sugar (I had been a vegetarian for years), pushed her arms up off of her chair, left for a few minutes, came back and handed me a lotion. She sat back down and said, "Put this on your chest one day, your hips the next, your belly the next, your bottom the next and continue rotating this cycle for the two weeks after you ovulate. Track your periods, use this, and let me know how it goes."

I was pissed. I wanted to take back every word of embarrassment I had just shared with this woman. Clearly she didn't get how severe my issue was. "You just handed me a cream," I said.

"Yes. It will help regulate your hormones. Try it and let me know how it goes."

"I want a pill. I am fucked up! How is a cream going to work?"

"Every single thing you put onto your skin or breathe in, goes directly into your blood stream. Shampoo, conditioner, cleaning products in your home, make up, all of it goes into your blood stream through your skin." There was a much bigger lesson in this than I'd anticipated.

I desperately wanted to trust her, so I left with my $40 bottle of lotion and within two days, my train wreck thoughts were gone. Sometimes, they showed up, but I was in control of them. The lotion worked, which was miraculous for my mind and scary for my body. I'd realized an entire life of a chemical infested body and cleaning products along with stress, had likely contributed to the illnesses I'd faced.

From the time Averiel was born until Aura was seven months old, which was three and some years, I had six unrelated surgeries (including two C-sections).

Pregnancy and childbirth don't just trigger repressed past experiences, crazy moods, and body awareness, they also significantly heighten spiritual awareness if you're open to their insights. What I knew intellectually but I didn't comprehend cellularly at the time, is, if you're the daughter of a daughter of a mother whose own daughter accused her husband of rape, you may unconsciously carry all of your grandmothers unresolved baggage and fears about not being able to protect your own, even from yourself.

What I didn't know cellularly then was that this story, likely from age four, may have made me the unconscious beneficiary of my grandmother's own desire to die since the day she blamed herself for her own mother's death in a fire, and her uncertainty of being able to protect her own children from her husband. The victimhood life cycle, cycled through me like a cyclone and it was me, not my grandmother, I'd assumed who's baggage, I was contending. I didn't know then that words, like stories, don't end when they're over. Much like history, they repeat themselves in our predecessors until the bravest of us are willing to win the war by giving up the battles we wage against peace.

Cleaning out of chemicals from my physical body gave me a motivation I had not had before. Set aside that by doing so, alongside eating more proportioned meals and breastfeeding, left me at *(a healthy)* fourteen percent body fat, I was becoming someone in the pursuit of true clarity. This time, because it was calling me, not because I was praying for it to call. All I had to do was answer the incessant ring, but I couldn't find the damn phone. All I could do was hear it.

My children's father spent the day chasing money and I spent my days learning, meditating, affirming, parenting, and present. My intuition was becoming louder than my fears as I gave myself permission to let it, via the practice of self-acceptance and teaching myself that unlike my fears as a little girl that every thought would have extreme external consequences, I was *not* my thoughts. Slowly, I was bearing witness to them in observation, like I'd observed the world, rather than claiming them *as me*.

He always told me I was crazy. Every time I asked a question, he deflected its answer in the direction of me being insane. He was rarely home. When he was, we fought, and I was at minimum one hundred percent confident he was having an emotional affair, though I'm about seventy five percent sure it was also physical.

My new self-talk was that I was a sexy, educated, sophisticated and driven woman living as a servant to two children in a life she was learning to explore with a man she couldn't trust. Driven toward what, was unclear, but driven nonetheless.

That's when I purged my life story in the bathroom of our house. For the first time, I was willing to get honest, instead of covering up everyone's tracks for the sake of pseudo protective peace. You'll never read the words I purged onto the page that day. The raw, detailed truths. Know though, that for those two days, I acted as a neglectful parent, locking myself in a room away from my children for as long as I could, to purge every piece of myself onto a blank space.

I went through it in puddles of tears, naked, surrounded by rolls of toilet paper and came out of it twenty times lighter in soul.

A couple months later, after a psychic reading sparked a heated conversation between me and my children's father, I packed up the kids and left. I was the first woman in my entire family so far as I could see, to ever leave a man I conceived children with. As the kids were getting older, our fights were getting heavier and if it were just me, I'd have played his game and won. But it wasn't.

They were there through it all and I was cognizant of them being enveloped in the same vibrations that I was raised on. Guilt, blame, and tension, even if it wasn't directed at them. *Always*, it showed up in the cracks between their father and I.

I gave up a luxurious life of getting by on scraps of the essence I wanted as meals, so long as I could stomach my partner, as a stay at home mom, in a five bedroom house with cats and a yard, and sweet daily freedom, to move into darkness, squeezing my kids back into the dingy, dusty, old room of my childhood memories. Not because I wanted to, but because I knew I needed to.

He didn't put up much of a fight. His fights were only ever to protect his image so when he did leave me with a special gem of wisdom, I was astonished he'd ever gave me anything real at all except my children.

He said, "Every time I ever made you feel crazy, you were right. I just didn't want to give it up. Always trust your intuition."

When I began to trust my intuition more than I doubted it, the world validated it back to me. What it told me to do was create a life that was different than the story I had written about it months before.

I enrolled in a life coaching program, began surrounding myself with a group of dedicated folks on a mission to open an environmental charter school in our area, and became wide open for divine direction. I had no idea where life wanted to take me, but I knew it wanted to take me more than I wanted to take it.

I vowed to become spirit led.

An amazing lover came along. He had just gotten into the area after walking across the country, from Venice Beach to New York City with his band. He was hot! He was the first man in my life I found myself irresistibly attracted to.

Hot artist guy just relocated from LA after a yearlong walk across the wilderness of the United States. Insecure girl coming off of a six year rollercoaster romp across the wilderness of stagnation, just relocated to the house of doom she had recently run away from. Great for expanding horizons, I guess.

We met at a raw foods cafe. In between every word he said, I whispered strange what-not affirmations to myself to override my undertones of insecurity. "He loves me. He totally loves me. I'm lovable. I am beautiful. He sees me. What's not to love?" While my mouth apologized for the recent weight I had gained, the fact that I lived with my parents, had two kids he should consider, and oh, by the way, I have herpes, my mind screamed *LOVE* at every thought that wanted me to be scared to face the truth about my circumstances.

By the time I left my children's father to the time I'd met my artist lover, it had been four months. In four months of living back in my old room, I gained *twenty five pounds*.

I had not changed anything at all about my diet with exception to the usual suspect of sneaking too many of my mom's homemade sweets into my gut. Other than that, my life had become one of raising my children by day. By the time my parents got home from work mid-afternoon, I walked up into the darkness of our stingy bedroom and didn't come out until they left for work the next morning.

All they did was bitch, focus on what *wasn't* done, you know… The situation obviously was not easy on any of us, including the kids. We argued constantly about the shit they fed them, about them undermining me or my parents speaking to them in a way that took away from their completeness *(you're naughty or you're a liar)*. This triggered me into an out-of-control spiral down the rabbit hole of my own fears that they'd be as affected by the world's words and actions as I was.

Maybe I wanted to play savior for my kids in those early years. Maybe I was still working out the savior archetype. All I did was defend their honor. The fight was exhausting. I shielded myself within four months in twenty five pounds of extra weight and my body returned to its habit of chronic illness.

Despite these circumstances, my sexy artist lover was designing me an engagement ring within a few months of dating. Indeed, he was also a silversmith and intended to make it himself. I was a novice to the principles of universal law, but when I was exposed to them, I immediately *understood* them, even though I was still conceptually, terrified to *live* by them. I'd have what Oprah calls, "AHA! moments," every time I stumbled upon information that felt like it'd been hidden in a room of myself that God sent someone in the world to turn the light on to.

My lover's presence opened me to my own desires. He was also patient with my bodily and sexual insecurities, taught me guitar, painted for me, sang to me, was a super sport with parenting tasks, and did a phenomenal job of acclimating me to his large, and very loving, close knit family. A structure in which I was not familiar nor comfortable with. They hugged me and I totally freaked out.

Once, I verbalized my discomfort while his entire family was dishing out hugs to each other, inviting me to join. We fought about it all night. *That* was an insecurity he wished I *would* hide.

He did not have STD's himself, nor did he care that I did. He researched them to familiarize himself with what he might be getting into, but decided that we were in it together. As a matter of fact, a good lesson I learned out of him letting it be, was that true love, was *not* actually conditional. He loved me, soul to soul. All other love I'd experienced had been based on physical appearances, or physical actions to sustain it, up until that point in my life.

He saw me through the layers it took to get to me and the fat that symbolized them.

I saw a picture of a brain once, with a finger sliding down the corpus callosum (the band between the two hemispheres) in a pleasureful manner, implying the corpus callosum was a clit to symbolize being intellectually stimulated. In such, the brain symbolized a vagina or indicated a pleasure center. Well, this was my life, on him.

He lived the life I wanted. He came home to settle down, found me, and his life was set in his mind. Whatever we did from then on, we'd do together. Except, *I* hadn't lived the life I wanted. Though he had lived it for me, having countless stories of serendipity, community, adventure, travel, and What the Fucking Fuck? moments, I was thirsty to drink them for myself. Living vicariously through him wasn't going to be enough.

We ate psychedelic mushrooms and ended up in ancient Japanese times as lovers once. In the scene that played along inside my head, we had absolutely no karmic baggage to work out. Back then, if it wasn't hard, it wasn't right. Not having anything to work out felt one, boring and two, important to remember moving forward.

A few months later, we got into an accident. A horrible one. A flipped SUV, me, hanging from the handle bars of the passenger window, while all of the shattered glass flew around, after just missing the edge of the cliff sliding backwards on our side, in the direction of opposing traffic. We could've/should've/would've died. He was driving. I never trusted him the same. Though he taught me love was unconditional, I made little wiggle room for him to unravel a mistake I perceived he'd made which could've gotten us killed. My part in this relationship was apparently conditional.

I went away to a challenging intensive weekend for my coaching program, came home, and with no justifiable reason, I left him. I didn't give it a second thought. I didn't understand why, but the message was very clear. *I had to do this on my own.*

Life between him and the rest is somewhat of a blur. I got jobs, lost jobs. Created community, lost community *(usually due to politics)*. Finished my coaching program, went back to grad school. Continued hating my living situation. Continued getting ridiculously sick and complaining about the confusion of my parents being both my prisoner guards and my saviors.

When Averiel was two years old, he sang me songs that "his two angels that came to his bed at night sang to him." I looked them up and they were actual songs. Lyric for lyric. I'd never taught him. It was a time I was home all day with them with no television. I killed my TV when I was twenty.

Every person I'd met who described themselves as intuitive or psychic referred to my son as being psychic. Averiel often ran out of rooms in the house, crying and pointing. Once he had a complete melt down and begged for me to go help the man he saw fly over the bridge in the "wash truck." He was hardly verbal for that incident, but was so adamant about his story he had me drive all over town, to every bridge, to make sure no one flew over it and died.

He pointed to pictures of my grandmother who had died while I was pregnant and called her by name. "Mommy. This is not my home. This place isn't where I normally live," came out of his mouth on several occasions.

I had an intense pathos energy once. You know the feeling that something horrible is about to happen or *is* happening and you're afraid to drive, so you call all the people that you love to make sure they're okay? As I drove anxiously, excited to get home for fear that we were all about to die, breaking the heavy silence, Averiel spoke out from the back seat. "Mommy, you died today."

"What do you mean I died today?"

"When you were Sophia's kids age you died when you were on a bike. Your bell on your bike broke when you were hit," he said. My niece, "Sophia's kid," was fifteen at the time.

"How do you know I died?" I asked. "I was watching you. I wasn't here yet. I was watching you from the sky, and you died." Immediately, the intensity of the pathos raised. I wasn't afraid anymore. It was a visceral release in the truest of senses. I didn't mentally dispel my fears, I felt them lift off of me as he finished his last sentence. As if he had released me of some karmic tie that was binding me to my fear in that moment, I felt comfort in his assertion with a response of peace to his claim.

Averiel threw another wildly bold statement into the air around that time. "Mommy, I didn't come to be with you. I came to be with Grammy. She was my Mommy when we were Indians. You were there too, but you weren't my family. When I was nineteen, I was stabbed in the back. I didn't see the man coming. That's how I died when Grammy was my Mommy."

Here's this kid I was fighting tooth and nail to protect from my mother and he's telling me he came here for *her*! There wasn't a lot of things that lit a fire under my ass to do anything other than jump, screaming wildly at my problems back then, but for some reason, that statement was one of them. It both enraged me and peeked my interest and I wanted to control it.

I'd gotten really into the law of attraction and began focused manifesting in hopes of getting the hell out of my parents house. I wanted to be *the mother* in the situation, not continually be fighting as a daughter in fleeting dreams of being a mother to my own children.

The school that came to fruition out of the community for an environmental charter school, offered me a job. I'd be making the most I'd ever made! *Twenty eight thousand dollars a year*!

Averiel was just about to be in Kindergarten and I swore to myself I'd do whatever I had to do, to never send my kids to a traditional public school. They'd previously had full scholarships to a Montessori preschool. I took the job, worked as a support teacher by day, a full time graduate student by night, was living in resentment and a blanket of thirty extra pounds and was perpetually, sick. I was on antibiotics for six unrelated reasons within three months prescribed to me by my *natural* doctors, that's how bad it was. *(They are MD's and ND's who utilize the ND route first).*

I was sick and tired of being sick and tired, but at every attempt to shine a light on how I could change my situation, I became terrified despite the fire that motivated me. I pitied myself for this reaction to a necessary change. Paralysis, as usual.

The last bout of those antibiotics sent me to sleep afraid, and woke me up to a clear, distinct, and authoritative voice coating the surface of my brain like kisses with its words.

"I will never not have money." After all, scarcity was what most of my fears and indoctrination came down to.

The only other time I'd had a visceral experience of a voice like this was in a sleep state as a little girl. Maybe nine years old, on a night I slept in my own bed, I sat on the floor of a yellowish, misty, house playing with a toy while people conversed around me. No one was talking but everyone was communicating and their communication was clear. I heard them but didn't feel the need to listen. Unconcerned, safe, content, I played with a pull toy until a man came over, extended his hand as if to tell me my time was up. I knew what he meant. I uncrossed my legs and stood up. Moments later, I was in a tunnel. There were two children floating around me. (If you were one of them, hello again!) All three of us floated peacefully, but rapidly, until a voice spoke. *"You are returning from heaven."* From my feet up to my head, I felt myself come back into my body.

I shot up the moment I became fully embodied and screamed for my mom. I ran to her bed, sobbing. I didn't know if I had a seizure, if I died or it was an omen, but what I was sure of is I'd just left my body, went to heaven, and was sent back. The voice in the tunnel felt as alien, yet familiar to me as the voice that woke me with the surprise of "I will never not have money."

Yup, that's what it said, clear as day, as I woke in the dark hours of morning. I smiled in the direction of the ceiling, called out of work, called a bank and in a puddle of my own snotty sickness, I walked into an office by early afternoon that granted me a mortgage as a single mother with two children on a twenty eight thousand dollar a year salary during an economic recession. I was twenty-five.

On one hand, it felt like I was giving my life away to a bank, *to settling*. On another hand, it felt like I was taking my actual life into my own hands for the first time. My *whole life*, not just my mental life. My biggest fear was leaping into giving my life away to freedom and that I wouldn't be able to sustain it.

I didn't tell a soul.

I dedicated myself to my healing in a full force way that day. No victimhood, only healing. The coaching program I was in stirred up my shit and made me eat it raw. The second week in, I ran into the bathroom, screamed at the mirror with mascara streaming down my face, splashed water on myself, looked again and said, "You've got to get the fuck out of here. You can't do this!" That's the general vibe of these times. I was stripped down, naked to my core, exposed to a world I didn't yet trust, and I had this perpetual feeling I needed to get the fuck out. Of what, I wasn't yet sure, though I was pretty confident leaving my parents' home was a stepping stone to recovering from self-proclaimed victimhood.

I dedicated my entire life to allowing my coaching program to be an investment beyond anything I'd ever let myself receive prior to it. Financial investment, time, physical, emotional, mental; across the board, I became a student of universal discipline rather than a master of rebellion.

Open, I was ready to be taught something new, which happened to be something very old.

I believed whatever I put in, God would meet me *more than half way* to take me to where I needed to go, so long as I took the first step. I promised to read up, dig out, work with inspirational coaches and leaders, and take physical care of my body in new ways beyond food.

Acupuncture called to me from a clinic nearby that afforded me weekly visits.

For the first few weeks of acupuncture sessions, I spent my days working, nights schooling, and every attempt in between to vision the house I wanted.

Limited thinking isn't something to get stuck in if we don't want to stay stuck. I didn't want to vision a life I could afford because I couldn't afford shit. I wanted to envision a life I wanted! Luxurious thoughts were my focus.

Ripping my hair out, hiding in corners at work, praying that all of my fears would be taken from me, acupuncture unleashed the wounds my body had stored, but my mind kept inarticulate. Acupuncture moved things from my physical body and the basement of my psyche, into an upstairs portion of themselves, which they'd never seen before. Much like giving birth to a daughter, acupuncture needled the threads of my stories and flooded my psyche with memories and insights about my lineage I knew I needed, but didn't want to be having.

A woman I'll likely never see again, after years of a time span that I didn't shed one honest tear because I was too walled off, apathetic, or terrified to break the levee of my own hell, sat with me at the most vulnerable request I'd ever asked for, while I laid face down, mouth dripping saliva, nose dripping snot, and eyes welling over with salty tears blurting out memories about my grandfather, the perpetual feeling of being unsafe, and the uncertainty of it all.

I still carried this impending notion that *I was crazy* or *they* were crazy and I couldn't be certain who it was. My mother always told me I made things up the way I wanted to experience them, so even in my victimhood, she deemed me a perpetrator. Hence, I was always terrified of myself. I never trusted them, or me, and if I was a perpetrator, I wanted to change. If I wasn't, I was a victim. If either were true, I wanted to change. As it turns out, change wanted me more than I wanted it and it pummeled me with its truths at times I wasn't prepared to get hit with them.

Change left me knocked out on the shore of my life, waking me up just in time to look over and see the next wave coming that I was about to take the hit from. The woman in the acupuncture room was with me in my first adulthood episode of pure, unadulterated and uncontrollably, raw, *vulnerability*. Every emotion of stupid, insecure, among all of the other bull shit we berate ourselves for when we end up washed up on the shore of our vulnerability in the presence of someone else, was drown out by my absolute need to become a puddle of my own unknowing.

Recovering stories and unraveling the meaning that my life had given to them wasn't easy to face. In doing so, I was ripping off layers of my identity, rocking a foundation and all of the walls I had built to protect myself from the world. I gave into defenselessness, but not without throwing a tantrum of sorts.

The labels I'd used to hold my story together were like shingles on a roof that was being ripped off.

House of fear has an address that can be postmarked straight to the ego and I lived there, wanting to go home. With a commitment to move out, each time a new layer of my story had *come to pass*, literally, was like a shingle being ripped off of the roof that'd previously held me comfortably in my discomfort.

Quite simply, it feels like death. Vulnerability is the first mark of the ego's demolition and love and fear seem to engage in a boxing match on its construction site. The construction site is where I laid on an acupuncturist's table, I'd never met before, unraveled.

The ego doesn't exist on its own. It requires us as its guests in order to be the host. I'd never left the house of ego even when it served me shitty food, made me its slave, bruised me, and told me I could never see the sun when I knew in my heart, if I just opened the window, I could at least *feel* it. It told me not to open the windows. Pissed off as ever, I listened.

Until now, which felt like ultimate betrayal. Toward whom, I'm unclear.

What I'm *clear* about is the house of the ego will not go down without walking through the doors of every township agency protesting its demolition. And its argument will be articulate and sound extremely practical. This passage is both fact and metaphor because I knew as scared as I was to own it, I needed a new house, and I wanted some sun. The sun sat in the corner of the room and listened to me purge in the form of a clinician. Still, a part of me was afraid she'd use my wounds to judge me and not to heal me. While the demolition of my house of fear was going down, I needed an actual home.

My realtor told me I was crazy.

My vision was of a house in the same town of my work at the charter school. I could feel myself walking to work with the kids on each hand. I envisioned myself wearing my handmade knit hat, a sporty vintage jacket, feeling the autumn air on my face while we walked to school together after an organic, wholesome meal, and being twenty pounds lighter. The house had to be on the opposite side of the train tracks from my work, have all hardwood floors, at least four bedrooms, and a fenced-in back yard.

The place I wanted to live reportedly has a ten billion dollar economy, mansions on the outskirts of town and had no less than a one hundred and *fifty* thousand dollar median average of houses sold in town. I though, was shopping on a one hundred and *fifteen* thousand dollar budget with commands to the Universe.

I told my realtor if she wanted to work with me, with the same audacity as if I was making her $200,000.00 off of the deal, that she needed to align with my vision and believe as deeply as I did, that getting what I dreamed up, was possible, despite her logic.

She complied.

Swearing off telling anyone in my family I was buying a house because I'd hear the, "You can't even take care of yourself's" and the "Where the hell do you think you're going to get the money for that?" but mostly the, "You're crazy! If you wanna be on your own so bad, have fun, we're not helping you! You're gonna see how hard it is in the real world."

We needed all the good vibes we could get.

Every one of those statements would've thrown me into a state of disillusioned panic, even more so than the same statements I was attempting to ward off that I was saying to myself. They always warned me about the *real world* and swore that they were protecting me from its effects. I was amped up to swallow that shit whole so long as the world just gave me a taste of itself without the weight of the fear I put between myself and it.

It was one of those Anais Nin situations: that "the day came when the risk to remain tight in a bud was more painful than the risk it took to blossom." I had to make this move, knowing both paths that could be taken in the transition would feel like a suffocation, one much slower and longer than the other. Obliging fear was not an option.

I wanted everything to be shiny and new, but I wasn't dumb. I avoided the drab house my realtor continuously asked me to tour for weeks, until I finally huffed in defeated compliance. It looked like shit online. After looking at a few terrible houses, I walked in the one I had been resisting, felt *free*, and said yes!

A few weeks later, without another adult witness, with no partner, no supporter, no visible net to catch my big decision, I signed a dotted line to my new level of freedom. A mortgage.

A yellow rose bud blossomed that very day in the front of my lawn. I called my parents, told them what I had done, picked up the kids from school and sat on my front porch in a sundress basking in the mystery I had just signed my future away to.

A month and a half full of work by day, school by evening, ripping out carpets, plucking up staples, taping edging, painting every wall, sanding, sparkling, and cleaning throughout the nights by my exhausted hands, I completed my vision. Friends helped some. So did my parents, unlike they vowed *not* to do.

I finished my room last.

The reprieve I experienced sitting in my bedroom alone, in a dark house I'd basically just gutted and designed with nothing but willingness, when I finished that last brush stroke of pale green, was the equivalent of being the most constipated you've ever been and then taking the biggest shit you've ever taken. The kind you want to take photos of and send to the friends who get you. Except, I laid in the center of my new bedroom, drenched in gratitude and reprieve with a feeling that not a person in the world could conceptualize the amount of letting go I'd had to do to get to that point. It felt so good, it almost hurt.

We had no air conditioning the first few weeks in the house during a dangerously hot summer. I was too afraid of bills to put one in. The kids and I, who were six, four, and twenty five at the time, limbs twisted together like pretzels, slept on the laminate kitchen floor under the only fan in the whole place, close to naked, dripping sweat, hair sticking to skin. Rugged, but free.

Immediately, I noticed a shift in the amount of time I was sustainably healthy. Though I hadn't used chemicals personally in a long time, we were surrounded by them at my parents' house. As if making the decision to be free, alone, made my body stronger, it was responsive to its new environment. I surrounded it with beautiful things, taking the time daily to revel in my gratitude for everything that was present in my new life.

The kid's dad still saw them every other weekend at my parents' house. I gave him whatever he wanted, always. After I left, he cut me off of health insurance, car insurance, and took back the only safe vehicle we'd had for the kids to cash it in and buy *my* dream car *(as a means of getting me back, or spite, still unclear)*.

We went to court, or I should say another version of a cleverly disguised hell, and he unleashed bullish lawyers with terribly awful threats when I had no lawyers or resources, and tied hands. He drove me crazy. Mainly because he wanted me, or at that point to hurt me, more than he wanted the kids. I knew his game and I resented him for playing it and for using my children as swords in his battle. That was a game I was too familiarly used to. When he pushed, I never pushed back, nor did I pull. Solid ground was the only place I could feasibly stand as the mother I wanted to be, but it was the furthest thing from easy.

When I met my shaman, the past life regressions I'd had over our first few meetings, painted a clear picture of the lineage beyond the lineage I'd already put together. Except, this time my children's father's role in it made complete sense in a way it never had before. So did my grandfather's.

I sat cross legged with my knees pointed to the sky, head dropped in between my thighs, rocking impatiently back and forth thinking, "This isn't for me! This isn't for me!" Native Americans circled around me at dusk, chanting a ceremonious dance on my behalf. Or rather, my daughter's. This life I'd tapped into during my regression was more clarity than I'd ever known in the life I was actually living here on earth, in present time.

I was angry. I felt like my people didn't listen to me when I knew in my heart I was never getting my daughter back. She was taken from me during a raid by white men in our village. I didn't see her being taken from me in my vision. I only understood the sequence leading up to the ceremony. After seeing myself agitatedly shaking back and forth like a scene in a movie about psychiatric patients (which aren't always terribly inaccurate), the facilitator of the ceremony reached down, pulled my hand and opened up a space in the circle for me to join their prayers for the safety and return of ours taken, including my daughter.

The scenery switched to images of me canoeing down a river, whispering telepathically to my daughter, whose name was Akeeta at the time, five years after she was taken from me in a raid facilitated by white people. I knew she was alive. I knew I wasn't going to see her again, but that she would know a full life without me in it. She was five months old when she was taken.

This information wasn't something I was imagining up. It was offered up through a well of my spirit without words and without doubt, but with much detail. I felt the glide of my bottom upon the canoe as it moved over the water. I felt my arms switch paddles from side to side. I had such distaste for the morals of the man that took my daughter, but felt actualized about it. I lived that entire life longing to share earthly experiences with a heart I carried under my own. Her arrival into the world was the most sacred blip on my timeline from birth till death, in that life.

My children's father in *this* incarnation, was the facilitator of *that* circle. Our connection in this life made no sense at all until I realized that by soul, we came together exactly as we intended to, lifetimes ago, to join a broken karmic connection. The seed that was planted in that ceremony, had sprouted our own uncertain connection as a couple of apparently opposite college kids whose only similar interest in this life, was getting fucked up.

The white man who took her from me in that life, was my grandfather in this life. Though my grandfather was alive for a few years after Aura was born, never for once, under any circumstances did I leave her alone in a room with him. Not once, ever.

The same man that is accused of rape, of extensive abuse, and sprouted countless amounts of shame and scar everywhere he went, was the predator I feared ran through my own veins from the moment my daughter was born.

I couldn't place it then. I couldn't understand if I was keeping her from him because he had molested me and I was repressing it all, or because I was feeling the sexual abuse triggers sifting through the threads of my DNA through my mother's flesh, or if I just didn't trust him after all of the stories I'd heard about him putting my grandmother or uncles in the hospital.

One thing I was sure of, even in his weakest hours, was that my daughter would never be left alone with him. This life, he didn't get to take her. This life is the first earthly incarnation my daughter and I have gotten to spend together. The gratitude I experienced at the thought of getting to share a life with someone I once lost, formulated a new kind of mother - daughter sacred bond between my daughter and I. Not missing a thing, taking all of her in, every smile, every complaint, every tear, became the message. Don't miss her when you have her. There was such a rapid shift in my paradigm at the fullness of this message. Be mindful of the extraordinary in the ordinary because the ordinary is extraordinarily divine.

I called my children's father, who would've done anything to tell me I was a psychotic bitch, to thank him for bringing my baby back to me. The information strangely delighted him.

That was just one dose of karmic clarity I tapped into within those weeks.

Another valuable scene played out with an atmosphere likened to scouting. I was a man in my mid-thirties at a time that the mid-thirties were equivalent to our current mid-fifties. Running across a log, summoning three boys behind me to hurry, we sprinted in our outfitter gear. The boys were teens, around fifteen. It was fall-like weather with leaves crackling under our feet as we rushed in an apprehensive desperation. The leader of the boys, I immediately understood that my concern was that *I'd let him go and he wasn't ready*. I taught boys to survive in the woods as a profession. As a portion of our training, we sent them out on their own for three days. My stomach felt like a helium balloon as we approached his body. I shooed away crows while I simultaneously fell to my knees and commanded the other boys quickly, to go get a gurney which was very makeshift.

He was my favorite student and was like a son to me. Scolding myself repeatedly for letting him go when I'd had doubts that he was ready, I wailed angrily at life when the other boys had left at my command. He was angry with me for not showing up to save him.

I was angry enough with myself for the both of us. I'd never had children of my own in that life, frequently thinking of him, especially in my older years.

That boy, my favorite student, is my father in this life. My father, a Vietnam tank commander, watched people he was in charge of die under his orders. As a Staff Sargent in the Marines, his orders were to never leave a man behind. Dead or alive. In this life, he watched people get blown up, shot, and all of the other disturbing war time's fears you could think up during his time in Vietnam. He did so, in a commander role. A similar role to the one I'd played in a life which he needed to forgive me for letting him down as his commander, shared together lifetimes before. He learned what it was like to be in the role of feeling responsible for the death of his men.

Here came karmic clarity.

Look, I'm not one to trust fluffy healers, psychics, or anything of the sort, but when they're right, when we're open, certain healers like the one I sought to become, can turn us on. Literally, like a light switch, we switch from being half dead, to all alive at the reception of being in *nothing more* than their *presence*. Don't think for one second that the process of my spiritual insight was similar to letting an obstetrician strap me to a table and slice me open to give birth to a child. Helpless, and out of authority. True healers weren't telling me anything I didn't already know, only shining light in a safe way on the things I needed to remember to heal, but didn't want to face alone.

A true healer is a spiritual midwife for our own birth, spoon feeding us ice cube doses of our own reprieve, encouraging us to spit out what they offer us that isn't *actually* ours into a bucket they hold for us in the moments labor hurts so badly we puke from the pain. All in one, they do nothing but let us see our own truth by being in theirs.

My shaman, my therapist as a teenager, my intuitive chiropractor, and pretty much every other healer I've ever resonated with at a soul level has said I carry a lot of sexual abuse in my body. When I was twenty-two at my first visit with a shaman, she said all of my chakras were completely closed except my seventh which is the chakra of connection to spirit, hence why I was always so sick. I was indeed, exiting the body on a soul level to escape the hurt of it, much like Miss Mammie Mae.

Except Mammie Mae was a master at reentry with purpose. I'd only mastered escapism.

The first time I met my shaman, she said, "It's as if you're sitting higher than your body and your feet are dangling about three feet above the floor." We worked around my fears of living on earth, the dark, dense place I fell into the pit of. Still, I never could quite upload a memory that made clear sense.

More memories did begin to surface, the deeper I got into my quest for uncovering what the fuck all of this meant. When I say *this* I mean, life, lessons, connections, my thoughts and memories.

Panicking with a feeling of *needing* to know what happened to me in this life that made me reject my sexuality so strongly, on a day that sexuality itself felt like it wanted to be resolved in me, I went to my sister's during a meltdown with many pieces of unfulfilled memories. Desperately, they wanted to be tied together into some formula that made sense.

Everything that came to me was questionable. Chewing on each insight in anticipation I'd soon find a worm in its bite. I wanted to be free of the apprehension of impending distaste for what life presented to me.

My sister very sternly said, "Why do you need to know who or what happened to you? What's it going to change?"

The answer is obvious here. I left her house and decided that rather than blaming them all for not protecting me from what it is I was searching to find, I would forgive them all, whoever *they* were, for knowing not what they did. Whoever they were, whatever hurt me, I would send love to.

Who was crazy though? Someone in this whole scene was still crazy and I wasn't certain it wasn't me.

I remembered the blue matted down carpet in my parents' room as I looked out the window into our backyard to see what felt like hundreds of people swarming in my yard in the perception of a four year old. They told me the party was for my birthday which also happened to be over Memorial Day weekend. I went into that room on purpose, even then. I proved to myself that no one was actually at the party for me. They'd tricked me into believing they were giving *me* a birthday party. No one came for me as I suspected. They were all drinking under the summer sun, music blaring, grills smoking, and I inspected their motives by seeing if they'd miss me.

No one ever came to find me in my hiding at *my* party when I was four.

I had to come out myself, which poses to be a larger than life, metaphor for the entirety of this story.

I already had two kids at this time and I wondered if they were busy handing out the same tests to life, to know if life was passing them, or they was passing it. I wondered if they were testing every circumstance to prove their worth in it, or its worth to them. As I had, indeed, they must be.

Language was always important in my mothering. I always offered two choices, never more or less. I facilitated talking stick exchanges between the kids during their arguments. Always open, honest, and bold, even in their youngest years. With a gentle truth, I wavered very little on what I said even when I wished I could take it back. All in all, my parenting skills were very conscious, which also opens doors to the reality that in all of my efforts for continuity, authenticity, validation, and unconditional positive regard, my children could very easily be misinterpreting my intent, or making up stories to justify feelings of their own inadequacy.

I really wanted to let go of the constant nagging idea that *one of us is crazy*. I wanted to feel the connections of truth and sacredness like in my past life regressions, and offer light to the relationships I had found only darkness in. The notion that my children could be growing up with the same feelings of "one of us is fucking crazy but I can't tell who's what," made me want to give up the story all together. Much like I soulfully understood when I was constantly distressed about the thoughts of my daughter being molested, by me or otherwise, I had to give up the story because I know stories in the mind, create themselves in space.

I wanted to give up the story to release myself from the burden of finding out who the fuck was crazy and to release my children and my mother from the same self-imposed burden.

Venturing into an honest inventory of forgiveness would have been much easier had my mother not been the same as she'd always been. Forgiveness is easier when someone is no longer hurting you, but it's an entirely different scenario to embark on it when someone is still blatantly and intentionally invalidating you. Giving it a whirl felt like the only way to begin healing.

Leaving the old pissed off, "why do I always have to be the one to change for the world" mentality, my journey started to feel more like it was a gift for *me* to change, than a gift to the world, though I know now that they go hand in hand.

Previously, I'd resisted giving into honest internal change because I wanted the world to apologize for what it had done to make me change into the fucked up mess I'd become. It never even occurred to me to allow *myself* to be the only one changing. I thought we all needed a change and I was sure I could change when *they* did. My waiting period was over, so I took the reins on the only change I could create. A new me from the inside out, into a me, far deep in the place I used to silently beg the world to see me from.

When we change, shift, and grow, vibrationally, so must, and so does, everything around us. This I've always known, though it didn't make me any more courageous to do it myself.

Intellectually, I really vibed with epigenetics and believed that shifting myself through energy, introspective, and soul work would be the equivalent of righting my DNA in the physical, on a ubiquitous time continuum of a family lineage that was fucked up way before I came to change it. As if I was sent here for only this one job, somehow changing the patterns in this family, began to feel like a God-given function of mine. Retrospectively, I believe it is also a God-given function of *yours*.

I'd found out that just like me, my own mother served her father and his girlfriends at a local bar she worked at and was also the bearer of her father's extracurricular affairs, set aside whatever he did at home to be kept secret. This pattern would not be repeated on my watch.

Secrets are the devil. Literally.

When we are in secret, we are keeping ourselves hidden and hiding the selves of others. When we feel so small that we have to hide, we aren't expressing ourselves in our truth and we'll never get access to our greatness. To be hidden is to be in judgment of the self. Judging ourselves is self-punishment, period.

With the realization that my highest value was freedom, which to me, looked like stepping away from the bindings of the seemingly unhappy and apparently scarce institution of *money*, came a unique surprise. My friends said if it wasn't for the fact that I had kids young, I'd be living in a tee pee in the middle of the woods somewhere.

The surprise? The woman I'd spent my life vowing to never become, shared the same highest value as I did. Freedom.

In her experiences though, money *granted* her freedom. I was bought things after she blind raged on me as a "lets kiss and make up" symbolism. When she was free of her blind rage, she dosed me with increments of the freedom she went to work for every day. Her freedom too, came at a cost and to her it looked like the corporate America I had equally sworn to disavow that she insisted I attempt to fit into. Only then, she thought, would I be free to get ahead in life.

My ideas of money came with a higher cost than the paper people placed value on. *Her* ideas of money came with a higher value than the cost of working to get what she wanted. The umbrella though, was that us two, incredibly opposite women, operated around the exact same virtue. Freedom.

I was open to find the commonalities in the experiences of my parents, the same way I would be open for any one of the patients, students, clients, or case studies I'd ever had at the time. It's so hard to allow for someone you've written a solid story about to grow beyond the story we've written about them. I was committed to first live into a *whole* new story, and then write about it one day.

The power of intention was my new best friend and there was one last thing I needed to prove to myself that all of this *stuff* wasn't *fluff.* Many of my repressions, lost memories, and insecurities centered around sexuality, so I got off of trying to figure out *why* and onto intending *what* I was going to do about it.

An Intentional Love Affair With My Vagina.

"Shit happens. Life is tough. Drink plenty of water. Stay away from mean people. Take care of your vagina. Listen to your gut. Learn to say "Fuck you, I'm awesome, smart, and beautiful."

—Twitter Meme

SURROUNDED IN SMOLDERING darkness, I pressed my feet into the earth and opened my mouth. The motion was so delicate, yet automatic I'd questioned who'd moved my jaw. The me that was witnessing from above, not from inches behind my eyes, smiled like if the color purple had a smile, would smile, watching it all go down.

Trust. She was watching me trust her.

Vibrationally, she was also letting herself be seen by the small me, that still frequented hell as her playground. She was power, *unhidden.*

Native American chants bellowed while my knees pointed to the sky, squished in between the wall of the sweat lodge, the coal pit, and two people on either side, combining our bodily fluids. Images of two Native American's pouring something into my mouth with a large wooden spoon filled my sight in the pitch black. I had a serious intention to heal that day.

This was the last of a series of mental, emotional, and spiritual exercises I'd embarked on in attempts to never have to tell anyone again that I have herpes and HPV. I also intended to never allow vulvar cancer to enter my body though my oncologist asserts that there is an eighty percent chance it will return throughout my lifetime.

I dug my brain into somatic psychology as a hobby, which sparked another memory. It was the summer after first grade. I peered out of the car window while my father was driving, realizing something unusual. "My stomach *doesn't* hurt," I thought to myself. I didn't notice when *it did,* only when it *stopped* hurting.

The discrepancy in the polarity of pain made me aware only when I wasn't experiencing it, that's how common my pain was at the time. I had no doubt the stresses of my childhood and my first grade year were the culprit of my never ending, undiagnosed stomach pains. That, or being fed processed shit far more than anybody should. Either way, I knew the emotional ties to my body went hand in hand with any other variable that could be accounted for.

I was putting together pieces of my body's puzzle. My nutritionist gave me a hair test with results that were off the charts. Knowing nothing about me, she said, "You must've had a parent that was exposed to Agent Orange." Some of my heavy metal levels were two thousand times what they were supposed to be.

Much like the realization that whatever I put on my body via the skin would go directly into my blood stream which automatically effects the physical body, and in turn, the emotional and spiritual, and vice versa, the realization that I was a walking result of my father's traumatic experiences came with deep trepidation about my own children's experiences. The physical idea of epigenetics taught me that my father's experiences likely flipped a switch in his DNA, thus mine. The switches that kept us cold and harsh toward life, I wanted to change.

Life became my experiment.

If my father's experiences could change my physical body along with my capacity for emotionality, I then, could change my own children's advantages in life by creating amazing and abundant life memories. Genetically, I perceived it could be felt in vibration, generations below me, and above. I chose to believe that my experiences, even when my father wasn't around, were silently and secretly repairing the DNA of lineages before me, including my father's. Prayer, of sorts that sent angels to transform my father back to his innocence in perception, by way of me living my life as a prayer for the benefit of our DNA and predecessors.

I wanted my body to be clean for the first time in my entire life. Daily, I affirmed safety mantra's about being comfortable in my own sexuality, loving a vagina that I'd been taught to hate, connecting in relationship to my C-section scars and stretch marks. I began touching my skin gently as a playground, rather than scratching post just to feel the boundary between me and life in a battle field. I wrote down the kind of experiences I wanted my body to have.

The day I walked up to the clearing where our sweat lodge was, as the facilitator feathered me down, I silently commanded, "Let this be the day that my work is done in this regard. Let this be the day that my body is clean of all impurities. Let me never again speak the words "I have herpes and HPV." If these viruses are still present, I ask you to take them now God, and I will vow to honor my body in ways I never have before, from this day forward."

Any rational person would be a bit weary over the delusions I was conjuring up. My *rationale* told me to stay out of it.

Again the script of *crazy* spiraled in my head. The vibration of my body felt clean, but my mind was muddied with doubts about being potentially delusional that anyone could actually heal themselves, especially me.

I kept my experiences to myself in confidence of spirit with doubt of mind. Six months later at a visit with my oncologist, I told him I wanted him to test me for herpes and HPV. He smiled at my faithfulness with a charmingly condescending squinty eye and said, "It's a waste of time and money. We already know you have these viruses and viruses don't go away."

With as much condescension as he gave me, I said, "I'm telling you right now! I've done enough work on myself to say unequivocally, my body no longer stores these viruses. You are only going to prove to me what I already know."

With hesitation and disappointment, he said, "I'll give you the most extensive DNA test we have. It'll show up positive at the slightest implication that you've ever even been exposed to these viruses, which we know you have, so again, it's a waste of time and money, but we can do it. My physician's assistant will call you with the results."

I continued to affirm that my body was clean. My affirmations transitioned from being images and thoughts in my mind, to vibrational experiences in my body. Affirmations that my body was clean were coming *from* my body, no longer from my head. What I was trying to attempt, was indeed, delusional, and it made me question my sanity at least a dozen times a day.

The call never came. Instead, a postcard in snail mail showed up with congratulatory negative PAP smear results. Unclear, shaking in anticipation, I dialed the office of my oncologist. They didn't forward me the results I was looking for.

Like opening a letter you know is an acceptance or a decline into the program of your dreams, I was ripping off a band aid in provocation of the truth. I was preparing myself for my illusion of cleanliness to be shattered, dare I expect to hear from professionals that *I'm not crazy.*

Dare I expect a miracle?

Funny to consider that never once do I remember picking *truth* in truth or dare. Always, I dared.

The woman on the other line was about as quick and cold as the nurse who called me to let me know cancer was a new acquaintance I'd be dealing with, *except in reverse.*

"Oh, Ma'am, everything was negative. That's why we didn't call. We don't call with negative results."

"Are you sure you're looking at the right records?" I asked as I anxiously bit off my cuticles, bloodying up my fingers.

"I sure am. It was all negative. Anything else I can help you with today?"

Jumping up and down, I did dance moves like a teenager in a chic flick after a first time phone call with a boy she's been obsessed with, quietly screaming her guts out into a pillow behind a locked door, hoping to discharge in a way her parents won't hear.

Ok God. I'll take it!

No person I'd shared with that I had STD's ever presented it like an obstacle for our affections. Likely due to my, "it is what it is" approach to it. Regardless, not one person cared in a way that allowed it to affect our relationship's unfolding, but I was ecstatic to never have to share the news with anyone again, just the same.

My only job was to let it be good, honoring my body's new vibrancy like I promised God I would do, the day of the sweat.

An Unplanned Pregnancy (Again!) Or
A Whorish Rebellion

"Every woman is a rebel, and usually in wild revolt against herself."

—*Oscar Wilde*

THE JOURNEY TOWARD truth when we dare provoke it, may wash us up on the shores to pummel us again and again, but the shore is of our own island and eventually the waves become our chosen friends. Not always easy to love, but always willing to play dare the truth with us.

A year later, a purge in perception yet again, lying next to a bathtub alone. I wrote this description of my reality:

I thought I was fine. I thought I'd be ok. In reality, I am fine. I'm still doing this. Tonight my son said, "Mommy~ I love you so much I could kill myself."

Why those words would ever come out of his mouth makes no sense on the surface. Actually, they're quite disturbing. Soul wise though, he was tapping into the unknown I was facing on the inside.

The next morning, *I killed it.*

On a Saturday night, I took a positive pregnancy test. I called the baby's father while my roommate and best friend of years, who I'd previously been in an intimate relationship with cooked us a hearty vegetable dinner.

"I'm so fucking pissed at you!"

"Why?"

"I just took a pregnancy test and I did NOT like the results. Go get me another test," total bitch like.

"Ok wait, you're pissed at me? Just calm down. I'll be right over."

Two more positives and a negative out of his box. I figured the more I took, the more chances I'd have of getting a negative result. I pranced around the house in my shorts and tank top talking on the phone with friends who I knew had abortions before, laughing, bitching I needed someone to get me stoned, while my friend cooked and the baby's father waited patiently for me to have a serious conversation with him which I avoided at all costs. I reverted back to being a fourteen year old version of myself in defenses.

I didn't want to talk about *his* baby in *my* body, or *any* baby in my body.

"I'm not pregnant. I will this away" filled my head for hours upon hours. Any thought that interfered, was quickly out-screamed by the last sentence.

No real responsibilities, this mother fucker is a touring musician. He explained our situation to my friend once, that being in my life is like this: "Imagine having five girls all at your beck and call. One you go to the movies with, one you consult for big decisions, one you only sleep with, one who's the house wife...well, I'm the housewife and I'm ok with that. I've always wanted to be a housewife. I play music, I come home, take care of the house, the kids, the yard. It works for me. It's all a matter of what you're willing to put up with. I do it for her."

We were living in somewhat of a polyamorous relationship structure at the time, though none of us defined it as that.

To him, this is just a mishap and his serious conversation entailed, "I'm not trying to talk you into or out of anything, but if we were in different points in our lives, we could..." I cut him off, shaking my head with an affirmative, "No!"

He wanted to talk about us. I'm wasn't ready for an us! I've got an us! A three of us! Three hundred of us (students) at my day job, an us meaning, *me, myself* and *I* doing an internship, working full time, writing papers, paying a mortgage, raising two functional kids, having a social life. He had weeks off, then he'd play in states I dreamt of going to and I resented him for missing me while he was away enjoying them. His life, was a whimsical spiraling upward kind-of-life where the outcome appeared to end with him on top, with very little effort on his part.

I was clawing my way out of a desert that just began receiving some rain for relief, while he was riding waves through life that felt to me, like gliding on a blue Hawaiian surf.

7:30 am Monday morning, I call the clinic. "You can get an abortion to-morrow if you come in for a consultation today." There' a mandatory 24 hour mandatory waiting period from the time between the consultation to the actual procedure. We'll need to give you an ultrasound..."

I don't want a fucking ultrasound. I don't want to see anything growing inside me that I am about to mutilate. Defensively, not wanting to look at the reality of this situation, *"just give me the fucking abortion! And do it now!"* went through my head as she went through her protocol.

What my mouth said was, "Well, I'm going on vacation on Wednesday so this needs be taken care of just about now."

I've always been pro-choice. Well, really pro-rights, and though intuitively I somewhat always *knew* I *would* have an abortion, I just never thought that one day, maybe, I'd *have* to.

My defensive behavior was proof that my unconscious was riddled in discord over my decision. This was one of those times that might be equated to bungie jumping when right before you're told to jump, you do everything to avert your eyes from looking down, kind of moments. I knew if I looked at this decision from anything other than logic or any time longer than a minute with myself, I wouldn't follow through.

I stayed busy until I went into the locked doors at the clinic. There was an "Are these people bothering you?" binder with names of all of the anti-abortion protesters who accost women and men at the clinic, sitting on the window sill that you must see before they unlock you in. I was beside myself. This had to be done, and tomorrow. I didn't want time to think about it, period. They did an internal ultrasound. I wasn't pregnant. They did two urine tests.

I wasn't pregnant.

All weekend I extended my energy *willing* away a pregnancy and I had.

"I will you away. I am not pregnant." were on repeat in my thoughts. I'd taken three positive pregnancy tests on a Saturday night, and by Monday my dilemma was made easy. I left the clinic, feeling reprieve albeit stupid.

Holy fuck! The power of the mind is astronomical! Mind over matter, really is where it's at. I'd willed away a pregnancy using intention. Well, a limited realm of intent, I suppose. You'll see why.

"People aren't like you. You can handle just being in an experience for a moment. No one else is really capable of living some commune-like lifestyle. You have to be gentle."

A line I'd heard about a hundred times during the years of living in some kind of open love life on a quest for experiencing it all, stretching my self-growth muscles. I challenged my jealousies, my ideas, my values. It is also the line I heard most when I shut out my unreal pregnancies father, who I did genuinely happen to love.

I laid next to him in bed naked, relaxed, smoking a joint, contemplating how balanced my life felt the night we conceived. I was a 26 years old teacher at a school I'd helped found, a year away from my master's degree, mother of the most amazing children I've ever met, which implied that I was raising them at the very least, beyond functionally. I was healthy, in my own bed with the power to kick out the man that had just stained my sheets with cum. I felt powerful in sharing myself with him. Sharing myself from a sense of owning my truth was beginning to feel like permission, as if I were finally allowed to see myself as free, but it wasn't yet an invitation.

He was almost too relaxed as I rapped the internal dialogue bouncing around my head out loud.

Then, *I felt it.*

He was going to want to sleep over. Panic set in. The man had spent the day with us, doing my dishes, mentoring my kids, and just shared a love-making session with me, and now I wanted him gone. I jumped to the cold side of my hot and cold tendencies, fast.

"I feel a snake right now," is what came out of my mouth trying to override my panic at his impending request.

"Really?" Then silence. Minutes later it came.

"Do you mind if I stay here tonight?"

"Kind of." And he was gone, until my "I'm so fucking pissed at you" call.

We deeply loved each other. We were real friends in our own very real way. A way that was palpable to most. We both knew if we streamlined our relationship into full time lovers, we'd want to change each other. We both had two very opposing wild sides, unattractive to the other, but alluring all the same, that we'd spend our lives attempting to tame. So, we let us be open which was *sometimes* confusing for us, but *often* confusing to the world.

The vacation I needed an abortion before I left for, was great. I got some serious bonding time with my kids, and unexpectedly, my parents. Though the afternoon of our departure at the age of twenty six, my mom slapped me across the face in front of my own children because I said, "What's the big fucking deal?"

The rest of the trip was cake. Magical actually. I supported my kids with boundaries I'd yet to set with my parents before. My parents intended days full of fun without breaks.

I wanted my kids to experience this in a relaxed way, for memories sake, not be drug through it imprinting the memory of being dragged rather than being bliss. Hell *is* the imprint of the drag.

When we got tired, which we did often, we left my parents and shuttled ourselves back to the hotel to sleep. I was seeing Disney World from a whole new vantage point. The morals of the stories were so apparent to me in ways they weren't before. Now, almost in truly psychedelic ways. Seeing the happiness of my kids brought me to tears daily. I was far more connected to them, the people around me, and life in general. That connection told me one very clear screaming message. The clinic was wrong!

My tits hurt. I was dizzy and nauseous every morning *(which I attributed to allergies)*. My body was preparing for something foreign, but I didn't want to look stupid by insisting on something I was making up. I woke up for work on a Tuesday morning, stopped at the drug store, picked myself up a pregnancy test, which the clinic told me not to bother with, assuring me my period would come. Locked in the bathroom at work, the test was more positive then it was negative. I immediately called the clinic.

"Ma m, we suggest you go to your family doctor. You're not pregnant. If you haven't had sex since the last visit, there's absolutely no way. Go see your family doctor."

"I'm sorry if I'm about to be rude, but this is something that should've been taken care of weeks ago. I've been pregnant twice before. I don't care what your tests say. I know my body and I'm telling you, I am pregnant! I *don't* need my family doctor to tell me that. You guys were wrong. It's very clear. I *am* pregnant!

I *was* pregnant! And! I want this taken care of. I do *not* want time to think about this!"

"Ok well, you can come in tomorrow. We'll give you a blood test."

"Well, will I be able to get an abortion tomorrow then?"

"Ma m, you're not pregnant, but we can retest your beta levels in two days and if they go up, then we could perform the procedure on Saturday."

They gave me an ultrasound. *Ohhhh baby*!

They never even bothered with the blood test. I scheduled an appointment as soon as I could, but that would mean I couldn't get the *twilight treatment* which is equivalent to being *put under* in abortion terms. I'd have to go raw. I decided I'd rather do it that way anyway. I wanted to make this a very conscious decision.

What my body was teaching me in its repressed memories, and its precise illnesses, was that what *I* didn't feel, my body still did. On all accounts, we can't get away from what happens to us, even with the greatest of drugs. Somewhere, the happenings live on, inside of us, waiting to be found out.

I knew my body would feel it anyway. Pushing away the pain with medicinal escapism wasn't going to take away the pain where it *actually* hurt.

If I was cognizant of the bodily pain and decision now, I believed I wouldn't drag out the emotional pains of following through with this decision. Painfully nipping it in the bud would ideally, lead to a greater bloom in emotional outcome. *Face it, hard. Face it now to move on*, was my motto.

Time had gone by which is what I wanted to avoid the first time I contacted the clinic. Just because the decision had already been made, didn't mean it was easy. I mean really.

I'm a mother. A nurturer by choice. I nursed my babies for three years, used cloth diapers, hung clean clothes on the wash line after washing them with organic homemade laundry detergent. I care! I love my babies. Which is *exactly* why I was making this decision. I wanted our lives to be easy and complete. Adding a third child with a second man, didn't feel anything at all like ease. It felt disastrous.

This baby was due on my daughter's birthday which was ironic because my daughter was due on my son's birthday. Any self-aware human being would find a sacred connection in this estimation.

In daily life, I listened to and followed faithfully every *sign* from the *universe.* Yet, I was ignoring all synchronicities when it came to this because they didn't support *my* decision.

I wanted this to be conscious, in my face, raw, and real, and the Universe made me face it, exactly as it was.

An unexpected girls debate night pursued over wine the night before I was supposed to go in for the procedure.

Two neutral, one completely against my abortion because she didn't feel I'd be strong enough to move forward from such a decision, and another who said, "You've made your decision, now get the fuck over it, move on, and never think about it again. Either way, no matter what, you can do it and never skip a beat. Keep it or don't, you can do it all." Battling both sides at once, coming to the conclusion that either way, I'd be killing a part of myself, in tears, I talked myself into the strength that night to follow through. I woke up confident.

Lunch time it was. Pulling up to my house from work, I saw him waiting on the top step of my porch. Grimly, he disclosed that his father had gotten into a motorcycle accident that morning, breaking both of his legs. This was eerily familiar to a friend telling me that a week after her abortion, which she dreadfully regrets, her brother, who was also her best friend, died and she has blamed herself ever since.

He had a gig that night, so right after this was over, he'd have to drop me off and drive out of state, leaving him no time to follow up in person with his hospitalized father.

I didn't even want him to go. It didn't feel safe. Who would even let me do this? Did he even get that I was about to have a tool shoved *inside* of my body to rip out a baby? My baby, well really his baby. Regardless, some cells that were naturally growing, I was going to have *unnaturally* mutilated and my body invaded while he sat in the waiting room, playing games on his phone. I felt like it'd be closure to our current relationship, but the thought that it might actually bring us closer scared me.

Sitting next to him, solidified my decision. He would want to change me. As a mother, as a woman, I was too wild for him. Wild in the simplest of senses, the way my father used to yell at me for walking in zig zags right in front of him. I didn't do it on purpose, my body's natural course was a crooked kid who preferred softness to edges and rounded to linear. That's how walking felt most natural.

I do things my way, and he wants them his way. Having a baby with him would've been more suicide then homicide in my eyes which may be reminiscent of my mother's own feelings toward my birth. I didn't want a baby to blame like my mother had.

Standing in the window, a long distance glimpse of me from across the room, evoked something in him. After I paid *our* dues, walking to my seat, he said, "Watching you in the window, you looked so good. If I didn't know you, I'd definitely want you. And did I ever tell you I have a thing for pregnant women?" I said, "That's great to say, now that we're here to kill our child."

He responded, "I never really looked at it that way." That felt almost as juvenile as my other children's father questioning the morning after pill.

Counseled by a young girl who looked as though she had about as much experience in real life as I do in mathematics, she wanted to talk about alternative options. I, however, didn't.

"Look, this decision isn't easy but I'm doing it. I want to take my son to Egypt. I want to share experiences with my children in Africa. I want to serve the life I already have, along with the people in it. I *do* want another baby, I just want it to be right, and this isn't."

She said, "Well if it's any consolation coming from the lady at the abortion clinic, all of that sounds great."

Thanks.

The actually procedure was quick. The counselor held my hand and I felt how deceiving looks can be. She'd been at this table before, and not just holding hands over it, but on it. I left thirty minutes after going in for the procedure, emotionally and physically wrecked.

The only lines I remember sharing on the way home were, "Can you please put on the music?"

"What do you want to listen to? Grateful Dead?"

"Sure. I don't care, just something."

All I wanted was my bed with some security blankets and the rest of the world gone. He dropped me off, closed my front door and yelled to my room,

"Call if you need anything." I slept the afternoon away, while my, very-support-ive-of-my-abortion-decision mother, took care of my children.

I woke up in the evening and drove forty five minutes to fetch myself some Thai Iced Tea and Pineapple Curry to eat in bed. Thai Iced Tea and Pineapple Curry accompanied by independent films in bed, and I wanted nothing more in the moment than having this experience *alone*!

A few hours later, my body thrust me into the most immaculate show of tears it had ever shed, literally. Nearly breathless, my pillow held my face while I screamed into it, face-twitching, snorting all over it. For *three hours straight*, (do not understate how long three hours can actually be) I screamed, my mouth curled under like a shy five year old trying not to cry out of embarrassment. I looked at myself in the mirror and asserted, "Suck it up you fucking pussy. You just saved your life!" countless times.

Every emotion of emptiness, insecurity, confidence, hope, possibility, vulnerability, and utter helplessness rode my neurons like a wave crashing against soft sand, but somehow remaining still at the nucleus.

My body searched for days. I acknowledged the possibility of it trying to compensate for the loss of its seed which it had so well prepared to bear. It immediately swung back into its familiar pregnancy place, in preparation for what was supposed to come. I had to admit that it was possible that I'd want to immediately jump into finding the perfect mate to bear children with and replace, as soon as possible, what had been lost, though I didn't want to admit it.

This was new for me. Being in the business of feeling a pressing urge to look for a partner had never been a profession I've worked in nor ever thought I'd actually consider. Things in these areas were supposed to flow with God's plan, but now, here I was, undoing plans and fearing I may try to force new ones. Almost superficial ones, like jumping into partnership and new motherhood out of fear of emptiness.

I'd read a great book years back about souls and their relation to abortions or the potential to be aborted before the soul incarnated into the physical body. The belief, which I did then, and still do hold as my own, is that the soul understands the potential for it to be terminated, physically, while it is in spirit, awaiting its time to manifest in a body.

What happens next depends on the way in which the soul is supposed to learn its karmic lessons. It will come back for a particular person, or to be in a specific place and culture in the world in order to best learn its lessons. If a soul is aborted, who came to be with a particular person, it will wait, and incarnate within that family again. If a soul is aborted who needed a particular atmosphere such as place and culture to grow, it will find another woman in that place and culture to come through.

If my baby was to be mine, I believed it would come back to me. Some could call this an *excuse*. I called it my *salvation*.

Three unrelated people who were not part of my daily life, contacted me to let me know they had dreams about me right after the abortion. Each of their dreams put me in a role of motherhood to three children. One girl described her dream saying that my youngest daughter was a girl, who looked just like my daughter. We were running into a basement escaping an impending tornado with our highest priority, getting the baby inside along with the rest of us.

Her description, having put a familiar face to my unborn baby, touched my heart differently than I'd been touched by the experience before. I suspected one day, I'd be succumbing to healing a wound I'd just sliced for myself that looked like an image of my sweet daughter's face but gone.

My body mourned the loss for months. My aborted-baby-daddy friend and I took our solid foundation of a friendship and slammed it in each other's faces until he got a girlfriend. The man that wanted me, was so scared by the sorrow I'd caused him, all he really wanted then, was a woman who'd never hurt him the way I did.

We slept together a few times when they were together which was liberating for me. Both of us actually. I think we took our love and just translated it into a bodily expression of play, rather than all of the idiosyncratic ways "true" lovers play out the "serious" side of love.

The new dynamic did leave me utterly confused. After a few explosive angry and sad outbursts in solitude, I wrote, and in my own writings, I saw the woman I was becoming. Through the eyes of my spirit, I realized how much the entire experience had assisted me in letting go (in the physical) of the things that no longer served me as a metaphor.

A message to my unborn baby:

"Seven months ago, my body reigned over me, once again claiming its defeat to the demise of a man.

Where pain precludes pleasure *but not for him*, for him, pleasure shoots itself out of a foreign appendage claiming rule over a valley beneath my belly button, stating, "I live!"

Pleasure exhales and the release leaves me empty but my body full.

The pulsing heartbeat on the white and black screen felt the closest thing to death this temple has known so far. I stood. I screamed inward the hate that has nestled itself throughout my vessels since my father found pleasure in my mother

A Queen now, I've claimed my body as my own, cutting out a princess undue to reign this land like a chef cuts fat off of steak

Either way, a part of me would've died

It took a killing in the most literal sense to feel how very alive I am and now "I" feel more like a choice than an obligation, and so do they, and so do you, and so does the man

I'm reveling in his pleasure now and demanding mine because my body is only mine, and only I can give it, freely or un-freely and it deserves to lunge outward the way men feel so privileged to lunge

You taught me that

It deserves no one but the Queen and from this worthiness, she so chooses her predecessors in their due time

I exist as I am today because of you and because of me, you don't

See you on the flip side kid

Thank you!"

Soon after, a shift in political direction resulted in losing the job that I was more concerned with keeping, than my unborn child.

I kept my head in my intellectual pursuits and moved forward. Typical pattern during times when denial feels like a privilege rather than a defense. Feel, nope. Think, intellectualize, definitely.

I reminded myself of what that voice spoke to me on the day I began my search for a house. *"You will never not have money."*

No job, no insurance, a mortgage, two kids, single and willing to grow, I gratefully opened an unemployment claim, contacted a woman in private practice I'd met years earlier at a star crossed lovers birthday party and landed myself a graduate internship at a private dance movement expressive arts practice.

Unlike the abortion, I knew now that if I depended on logic, none of this would work out. Ignoring all logic of how we were going to survive, I committed more deeply to healing. My relationship with money was in the gutter. If I didn't fix it, I knew I'd come out of this poor.

To sum up how it was supposed to go in my mind, I wrote a story, as I often do when I want to create something in my life.

A simple version of how I wanted this terrifying time to go went like this, "I want to work less, learn more, come alive, and come out of this time and apparent struggle, richer than I'd ever been." That was my story and I was sticking to it.

Un-Grinding.

"Had I not created my whole world, I would certainly have died in other people's."

—*Anais Nin*

I WATCHED MY parents work their whole lives with constant complaints about not having enough to show for it. Since I was fifteen years old, they watched me do the same. I repeatedly lectured them, with reasonable articulation, about quality of time being more fulfilling than the pursuit of the grind. The grind didn't guarantee a thing but they devoted to it like a religion. In a promise to let myself experience presence in my life, I swore to not let myself conjure up a next step. I would sink into a life that felt like a vacation for the time I was allotted a steady unemployment allowance which would at minimum cover the mortgage.

My internship was only two days a week, which left me a lot of free time. For the first time in my life, I swore off all pressures for the pursuit of knowing presence, the way I'd barked at the world that *they* should do. I was pretty certain if the world relaxed, then I could relax. An experiment in the magnitude of true personal change was what this was about. Through all of my *should's*, scarcity thoughts, doubts, thoughts of being the lazy, unworthy, the spoiled brat my mother always said I was, I would find a way to relax.

If I was going to hit bottom with money, I wanted to enjoy running around on ground zero just to prove to myself that money wasn't really the thing my life was after. I wanted to test my tolerance for feeling rich when I was most poor.

The martyr in me loved this. I've always had some sick devotion to suffering to prove my reverence for God. How that makes sense, I can no longer relate to, but it was my sacrificial beliefs of always suffering consequences if something good comes, that I built my identity on.

The moment *good* came, I hoarded it, stored it, feared it, and told it I loved it manically awaiting the inevitable doom that came with its presence. So much so that I never *felt* it be good when it actually was. I only waited for good to show me the bad that comes when good is gone.

Challenging myself to change these ideas by continuing to expect good at a time when it appeared my entire escape plan into the life of me, as a woman, might backfire, became my objective.

Indeed, I might end up right back where my mother swore I would. Under the thumb of her fears, under their roof due to yet another fuck up at the mistakes of her daughter's poor choices.

Presence takes practice when you exit life in the grind. Appointing presence as my teacher, I became its student and not always so humbly. I oscillated between having to tuck myself under my covers to stay in one place to overcome my impatience for stillness, to hiking miles a day, touching every tree within arm shot of the trail, just to keep myself from manically searching for the next step in "real life." I distracted myself with positive, ideal thoughts instead of giving time to worrying about how I was going to put organic food on our plates.

With all of the shifts that had taken place for me, I felt like a whole new vibration of myself that I vowed to bathe in. Knowing who I'd be if I stopped responding to life by fighting, running, or charging life like a super woman, was uncertain as ever, but I wanted to know her. Life was asking me to let it be, to give up forcing, and let go of judging *should's*. It wanted me to experience it in the position of a guest in a mansion, rather than a host in a frat house. Learning how to be a guest to life's indulgences was an alluring quest as I'd always felt I was the one dishing out indulgences somehow, staying pissed as ever that life didn't return the favor.

Despite extremely limited resources, I prioritized my personal evolution, finding creative solutions to see my healers, got scholarships for workshops at ashrams, and didn't compromise on organic foods and products. We didn't have health insurance, so organic food was one of my top priorities. It was the only health insurance we had.

Still carrying around the extra pounds that shielded me from my reality of having to move back into my mother's house years earlier, I dabbled in filling the silent moments with magic. Physically, I looked so full. I was healthy, and always proportionate, but thick. I still got scared staring at my ceiling for hours, like I did the first time my children's father left me in empty wonderment, but the episodes were shorter, and somehow more healing. I was building this foundational life on the outside. A life I'd just gotten an abortion to invest in.

I'd healed myself. Gotten clean. Bought a house. Gotten educated. Traveled a lot. Tapped into endless amounts of extraordinary in the mundane. Yet, I was still searching for what I'd already found. I only knew searching. I wasn't ready to give that up.

Who I was without a constant nagging feeling of having to find my incomplete pieces was a complete unknown. Even in my most present moments of meditation, I'd ask a question, always seeking, never withholding my mind to fully feel what was going on in this very moment. The *peace* right in the moment, was simultaneously the only thing I wanted and the only thing offered to me, and still I found myself searching elsewhere in my mind to know peace. I was missing the point. The point, wasn't missing me. That much, I knew.

On every mirror of my house, I wrote kind things to myself in expo marker. I dabbled in feng shui, invested in a full house of plants that I vowed to keep alive as the healthiest versions of themselves. I created my life as a reflection of what I wanted to be because my body certainly, was not the way I wanted it to be. If I over-identified with it, I'd be missing its point: that it was here for me to experience *myself*, not *it*. It was my car, but the power house that smiled the color purple at me in the sweat lodge, the one who'd been hiding, was the driver.

My neurosis wasn't going away, but it was quieted by kinder words than I would've heard from it before. The difference I could see in the conscious commitment to practice healing in spite of all else, was that my depressions lasted for a day, rather than fifteen months. My highs let me experience them more fully without such a sense of distrust for their reliability and consistency. And, my crowd was thinning. My life was becoming quieter which felt lonely in my guts, but still in my heart.

In one of those times when our whole body feels weighted, like a black and empty void that's trapped inside of itself, I saw my shaman. I was really there to work through something I haven't yet mentioned.

A several years long, dangerously unflattering obsession with the motives of my star cross lover. I met him two years after I left my children's father. He fit right into a symbol of a life I would've led at our age, had I not had children. He, like the father of my aborted baby, was a musician. A smooth charmer. An open heart with a soul that makes you want to preserve it because in its presence, everything feels so crystal clear. Except, it never was.

A very long story short, our love will never be defined by a story or minced into a time frame. But *my* love, was just getting a sense of rattled taste buds. As with anything else, I paid attention to very little unless it was slapping me across the face. Rather, I was missing what was in front of me, in search of the hand that may potentially be slapping me if I let myself pay attention to anything but it.

Ani Difranco says, "For every hand extended, another lies in wait. Keep your eye on that one. Anticipate." And that basically summed up the entire way I looked at the world, specifically in the realm of intimate love. I always had a back door. Always a plan B, and C, and D. I took every success, challenge, and defeat, *as a challenge*, and found an infinite number of problems that could be solved. I appointed myself to solve problems that didn't exist, thus somehow always inadvertently created them.

Though I was living a life surrounded by incredibly loving friends and a few intimate sexual partners, I didn't let a *body* get close to my soul. *That*, was preserved for *him*.

Strangely though, I always hid from him, even in my presence. He was in. He was out. He'd show up, we'd drift off into some terribly uncertain adventure of a time for a few days, sometimes weeks, and then, he'd be gone. He never hid his affections, though he never committed to them being the same tomorrow, nor did he completely own them. Our ambiguity felt the same as feeling kept for torture, with a questionable belonging by my parents as a child, always in the grey, never in the black or the white. He provoked the same insecurities I'd had then, though now, I was intellectual enough to seek control of whether this would end up in the black or the white.

We both had enigmatic and mystical names for ourselves in the love department, and together, we were like two magnets chasing each other from the opposite ends of the sides that would fasten us together. We just never got it right.

Or rather, I just never let go of the idea that there was supposed to be a *right*. Ours was a case of when two *rights*, don't actually make *it* right.

Certainly, we both circled each other in the periphery of our pride's boundaries. We kept it open, both cowards to cut it or tie it. We left it hanging. So, I fucked his friends. One, because we all truly did and do love each other as people. Two, because, I desperately wanted to come up with something exaggerated enough that may hit him where it hurt, so he'd be bold enough to finally end me. Grey hurt. Surely, fucking his friends would show me if we belonged in black or white. That'd be a great way to end this uncertainty. Duh.

Love like that is miserable. Bittersweet and as he calls *me*, a combination of dark chocolate and super fucking hot peppers. He never did do me the service of cutting me off.

Years of being in love with our highest potential, of not being able to wash his scent out of every trail I hounded down, I landed on my shaman's table hoping for a final reprieve.

Besides the male and female cardinals showing up outside her window when I was there that indicated to her, I would soon be with *my person*, the session didn't provide me with the reprieve I was looking for.

The moment I laid down, she said, "There's a baby here, attached to your right hip."

Mind you, I hadn't seen her since before my abortion. The last time I spoke to her was at a time when my throat was so banged up, I could barely speak for about a month. I wasn't sick, but locked up vocally.

Without seeing me, she called and left a message saying, "I see you hanging from a noose in the woods. This point in your life is clearing a past life in which you died by hanging." Her words exported me to riding in the back of my mother's metallic light blue Ford sedan as a little girl, ducking behind her seat every time we went by a section of woods by my grandparents' house. I saw myself, and other women in bonnets. It looked like colonial times. I knew I'd rather die for something I believed, than live for something I didn't in that life which smelled strangely familiar to now. That's why I was hung. A lot of us were hung. I wasn't the only one hanging in the woods.

For the same principle of being unwilling to stand for something I believed was failing, I'd recently lost my job. I never even called her back to tell her my experience of seeing her vision or of the immediacy that my throat cleared after her call.

I looked up at her standing to my right, her hands on my hip, and exhaled a breath accompanied by tears. "Is there? Is she still here?" my face quivered.

Telling her about the abortion, we ceremoniously released my unborn child to my spirit guides and angels. An uplifting sensation on my right. To my left, visions of an angel holding my scared, uncertain, lonely little baby who'd stayed with me until now, filled the space in the room.

Realizing what I'd done, this souls connection for the first time, felt like a living, breathing, entity and I wanted to know it.

"I want you sweet heart," I said. "I just couldn't do it with him. It wasn't the right time. Go with my angels now, and together, go find your father and send him to me. I promise next time, you can come through." The soul came for *me*, not my location. This, I knew.

I felt its presence. It was honest, and vulnerable, uncertain, yet strong and determined. I promised to get to know it earth side. I trusted it had a job to do. I wouldn't carry another child with a man I would leave. I wouldn't carry a child with a love less-than-unconditional. I wouldn't carry a child for the sake of distraction or motivation. I wouldn't carry a child under scarce conditions, nor would I bring a child into this world to go back into the grind paying someone else to raise it for me. The only way I was going to bring a baby into this world was for the sake of itself, under happy, healthy, relaxed and loving conditions, and I swore it.

I also swore that despite what doctors had bucked against, the only way I would birth a child again, would be *naturally*. High risk according to medical terms or not, the only way out for any other children of mine, would be through the canal, not by a surgical knife.

Visions of the most empowered version of myself giving birth in a sea of dolphins on a quiet island cove, tumbled through the stones of my unconscious. Logically though, it could never happen. Vaginal births after cesarean are already *risky* for medical doctors, and the seizures, though I'd learned to breathe through every impending attempt my body displayed of going into one, were still a concern on the back burner of my adventures through life. My natural doctor told me I was too high risk and that I'd never find a midwife or an obstetrician that would take me on.

Telepathically, I sent a strong message of qualifications and trusted the power of spirit to align my desires if the soul wanted to come back through. I trusted deeply that it would, when I gifted us *both* with the blessing of genuinely *letting go* that day on my shaman's table.

My angels and guides were in charge now. I freed myself from the bondage of a decision that unconsciously, I must have considered a cosmic mistake. I said, "See you later. I love you," to my unborn baby, believing that the next time I connected with it, it'd be showing up, earth side.

Letting go, for the first time, felt like receiving rather than sacrificing, which was translating into other areas of my capacity to let go.

I was always a coward. I waited for others to push me out. Everything was extreme. If I didn't want to date you anymore, I wouldn't tell you, I'd fuck your friend and make you leave me. If I didn't want to be your friend, I'd silently sever our ties, hoping to slip through the back door, unnoticed.

The only job I ever quit, I quit because of an extreme human injustice I couldn't condone. A month later, the woman I quit my job over, was fired. Every other job I'd had, somehow never ended. It just smooth transitioned me into the next phase. Positions or entire companies I worked for got bought out, giving me the choice of unemployment or to work as something different with another company. I didn't do well with endings. At the smallest and largest of gatherings, I'd leave without a goodbye. Parties of my own, would send friends on searches for me only to find me sleeping in my bed without a word of my exit. Boundaries weren't my thing. Endings made me cry. I didn't trust beginnings not to end, so both were a fresh boundary indicating change that left me uncertain of whether I belong inside or outside of its fence.

A year of working less in the physical world, paying more attention to actively constructing my inner world, and utilizing the tools of the spirit world, was teaching me that boundaries aren't punishments, as I'd known them to be. They weren't the impending slap across the face that happened when I didn't know I did something wrong. They were just fences indicating demarcations of what was acceptable. I was learning that I was allowed to put up my own fences. Putting up boundaries, wasn't me slapping people unexpectedly as I'd previously thought. It was me claiming the territory of my life and the conditions I would accept into it.

Without boundaries, everything was an invitation into my internal universe. Boundaries, though I felt very much like an apathetic, ruthless, hurtful cunt when I set them, even the smallest ones like, "P*lease don't eat the last of the hummus. I just bought it for the kids*" to a visitor, felt like a feat in battle, but I practiced them anyway.

Practicing boundaries seemed like there was a potential outcome for a very lonely existence. All of my friends were old friends. Friends whom I'd been through hell and high water with. Friends we babysat their baby siblings while their parents shot up. Friends who paid their fathers mortgage at fourteen from working as a server while her dad was secretly in jail after her mom said she was going on vacation four years earlier and just never came back. Friends who knew heartache and survival like the back of their hand. Friends who's attempts to control our relationship and their lives came from a well-intended place of extreme displacement.

It's a blessing to share a history with people. It's a blessing to grow up beside others, but our common denominator was ultimate protection. We protected each other then. We proved our loyalty through blood, sweat, drugs, and tears and vowed to do it forever because we were the only ones we believe would.

It's not a blessing however, to use a common denominator of protection repeating patterns based in fear, when there is nothing any longer, to be protected from. That's what we did.

We recreated things to have to protect each other from. I wanted new, fulfilling relationships of celebration and fun, of life and spirit, not of dissection, problem solving, and game playing based on the survival of our egos.

As circumstances came and went, my heart decimated and shocked back to life, countless times through the insights and steps I took that year. I weeded out, pretty literally, every relationship I'd had in the life I'd known before it.

Change doesn't come from meditating or sitting behind a computer screen, listening to someone tell you how to change your frequency. It just doesn't, though I wished it did. Every "I love you" I wrote to myself on my mirrors would be meaningless if I didn't back it up with the actions of self-compassion that opened me to the text book of its teachings. Practicing daily affirmations, mirror work, meditation, gratitude, yoga, writing, and anything else imaginable, was only the *cover* of the book to progressive change. Daily *applications of living*, are the *body* of the encyclopedia of change. I wouldn't stop until I read through and could spew out every one of its pages.

Gut wrenching, feeling like whether I was going to shit or vomit all over myself or not, when my intuition said something, I listened, even if my ego awaited the consequences. The thought of the life I'd have after I cut most of my ties to my past never really crossed my mind. I only intended to follow my guts and keep my ego out of it.

My mother and I maintained the same kind of relationship that we'd always had. She belittled me, I sunk into myself, and brushed it off, encouraging my empathy to feel her suffering to justify her actions which I wouldn't recommend *(in retrospect)*. Shame can be met, without feeling shame for stopping it, shamelessly.

She loved to jab at me *to my children*. The slightest scent that she was the same way *with* my children that she had been with me though, I lost my mind on her like I did when I was thirteen. Like when she told my *healthy weight* son who was in fourth grade she'd give him fifty bucks if he'd lose ten pounds by summer. Or when she told my daughter that her dad made a blatant decision to not see her as often as my daughter would've liked, so she shouldn't feed into her daddy issues by praising him, *when she was seven*. Still, just as I was a buffer in my parents' relationship, though she was sometimes harsh with my kids, she averted most of her attention to *me* and *my* mishaps, which I could tolerate at the time.

Obviously, an educated, self-sustained, evolving woman who got her own house, and works tirelessly for advancement in life, in this situation, would consider never speaking to her mother again. In my desires to be tolerant and compassionate, my constant struggle laid in the foundation of my forgiveness work.

Damn it! I forgave her, but she still did what she always did. She gave me more and more reasons to forgive or oversee the angst she spewed all over me. How one accepts tirelessly, something into their life, for the sake of martyrdom and overcoming, that continues to eat away at their soul for their entire lives, who is also *seeking peace*, I will never find out.

"You'll never be married. No one would ever want to marry you."

"You're a wanna be."

"These people can't seriously like you. You're deluding yourself."

And the kicker was always the money tie in. She'd drop off clothes and food that though I didn't ask for, I was incredibly grateful for. Then, she'd remind me that she did it, followed up by a few desecrations to my character about laziness, not doing enough, and that I couldn't do any of this without her and very soon, she was going to stop giving us things. You know, one of those kind-of-exactly-like-it's-always-been Groundhog Day moments. Her in charge of gripping the hair right at my scalp and shoving my face under water, only to let me breathe and tell me I was breathing at her grace, by her hand, and without her, I'd be drowning because I'd be too exhausted from wading in a pool of my own shit.

I'm not one to force my kids into anything. I know how unwell that turned out for me. So the day my daughter didn't want to go to girl scouts and my mother barged through my door screaming at her at the age of seven for being a quitter, I defended her right to stay home. My mother was screaming when I saw *the look* and told my daughter to go to her room. The look my mother had, only I know the consequence of.

My mother chased her up the stairs and tried to drag her out of her bed by force, slapping her legs at my daughters resistance. I lifted my daughter up, screaming at my mother. She hit my daughter through my arms. For the first time in my entire life, I set a boundary with my mother and I meant it.

I told her to *get out of my house.*

Hesitant, still. A woman who'd just hit my child for nonsense, I was still hesitant to mean, with conviction, that she *had no choice* in the matter, but to get out. She listened though. Of course, she called me immediately to tell me she was coming back and I was irresponsible. I stared at her number on my screen while I cried on my couch, not upset because my resilient daughter had been through a ridiculously unnecessary and potentially destructive situation, but because I knew *meaning it* would be a whole new standard of my relationship with my mother that I'd been afraid to know. I was scared for myself, and I was sad for *my mother.* All she knew how to be, was exactly what she was. I was no longer begging her to change. I'd love her, or I'd leave her. Period. This ambiguity of belonging shit was going to turn tables in my favor. It had to.

I'd begged her multiple times to be a mother to me. In each instance, she responded mercilessly that it was tough shit, she's who she is and who she is, doesn't like me, nor does she want to have a healthy, loving relationship with me. The last time I sat with her, pleading her acceptance and affection, I was twenty seven years old. I swore I wouldn't do it again.

Change was no longer on the table, but progress was. To take it by the horns, I set out to put a stop to these kinds of dramatic, sickening exchanges in my life.

Boundary number one. I'd had claimed territory over my space. Up until then, the kids and I lived a life with an open door policy. We never knew who we'd come home to in our own house. Our community had become our chosen family, and slowly, but surely this was the first signal that we were transitioning into an invitation only kind of life.

With the help of food stamps and gratitude, my bills were paid and on time over the course of that year. I graduated my masters degree with a 4.0 GPA. The first thing my mother said when she saw my diploma in hand, was she was going to write a letter to the teacher who'd told her I'd never be more than a C student in first grade to prove that bastard wrong.

A Master Of What With A Masters Degree?

"Follow your heart and intuition. They somehow already know what you truly want to become."

—Steve Jobs

AS I RELEASED situations that kept me stuck in the dissonance of my head and my heart in my personal life, synchronicities were happening within my community that were guiding me into a business in private practice. A masters degree in psychology doesn't prepare you for anything, except being a clinician. Business, not included.

I'd begun getting this whole relaxation thing under way. Business, like a steady, lifelong love, was not in my cards as far as I could tell. Truly, I didn't want it distracting me from my *real* work either. *My inside job* is what I truly wanted to master.

A directionless, recent graduate in attempts not to sell out on my new insights and the integrity I wanted to keep with them, I wrote about life like this in my morning journal:

As an American, especially of this generation, we are hard pressed to adhere to the standards of *wants* that are apparently the inherent nature of our society. What do you want? What are you going to do? Well, as an individual in an individualistic culture, I was hard pressed to address these issues within myself. What if I want for nothing? Obviously, this seems almost irrational, but really!

What if this whole life, I've been seeking and searching for the things, people, and situations I want and all the while I'm left utterly confused in my indecisiveness? What if I'm entirely decisive? Not making a choice is a choice, right? So, what if, it's not that I can't figure out what I want? What if, I just don't want anything? After all, the select few things I've been focused on have always come to me readily and easily. The attachment that comes from seeking and searching for the *wants* America tells me I'm supposed to know, have left me bewildered and confused without reason.

I've set goal after goal, reached them and set off to overcome the next. Specific focus in matters of the physical world, like jobs, educational hierarchy, material goods, have served me well. But in matters of the heart and wholeness, paying attention to these goals has left me depleted and un-actualized. Distraction after distraction has fostered an imagination unimaginable and given me the freedom to explore the desirous realities that may never come to fruition in matters of the heart.

I'm considering that the egg came before the chicken because often, whatever it is I want, has presented itself to me like a ghost dropping change around your house. I didn't realize that I was even missing something until I got it. It's typically not the other way around for me. I'm not one of those, "you don't realize what you've got till it's gone" kind of people. I'm an "I didn't realize what I didn't have, until I had it," kind of person. This is something I often forget though.

The empty spaces leave me hungry to fill the voids, but I don't often have a particular *object* to employ. In times like these, I flounder like a soul fish floating around inside a dark cave of a stranger's human body, noticing the vastness within myself without any clear direction. Then, viola! Something comes and I find it colorful. All things keep adding up and then, in the ebbs and flows of life, the added up pieces manifest the most complete version of myself.

Since I was 18, I strove to be complete within myself, possibly before that, as a birth right, but the choice became a conscious one then, fostering a knowing, of the most independent version of myself. Self-work that has led me to bright lights and black holes, has left me triumphant and empty and meaningless and provided me with moments of purity that could never be touched by another human being.

I used a city driving move in the non-city. The already suspecting driver called me a "fucking bitch." I winked and smiled in my most condescending sense of self and wondered, if I'd actually gotten anywhere. On the inside that is.

All of this self-awareness intended as the preparation for the rest of my life has lead me to an ultimate sense of self-preservation, which by nature is success, by nurture, absolutely meaningless. All is lost if not for the enhancement of genuine, open and heartfelt relationships. The kind that two bodies intertwine next to a stone fireplace during a snow storm in an A frame log cabin that provide the warmth that only the intangible space between, that thing called love, *that* kind of warmth, can bring. I guess where I've gotten is a place of knowing that all this work is only preparation to drop the self-preservation piece and share experiences of awareness with another in love.

It's like the ending of *Into the Wild* where he implies all of his pursuits to find himself were meaningless without relationship, after his entire adventure, he strove for an understanding of himself, *as himself*, but how can one possibly do that without the mirror reflected back to them of what they are *experienced as*? In love? I guess I've gotten nowhere, but where would I be had I done one thing differently? Not sure I'd want to know.

I was raised to "never depend on a man." To depend on no one.

I wasn't in any position to make any kind of executive decisions about my next steps nor was anyone stepping in to challenge my notions of dependency. The only solution to this uncertainty was the good old, let go and let God mantra. Just as I took the time to squeeze myself into the present moments of my life without feeling trapped by them, I promised to squeeze myself into God's plan for me, rather than squeeze God into my plan.

A healer, that's what I am. A healer because I promised to heal *(myself)*. I was definitely not a business woman. My financial status was below poverty level and I was terrified to look at my bank account or any account for that matter. I felt grossed out by people in suits, and I still didn't value the institution of money. Along with feeling the richness of true presence, money was becoming less far out of reach in my mind, which translated into my life. Life in business, I assumed, would look like giving everything away and martyring my self sacrifice in my not so spare time, wallowing in self-pity.

For life's own reasons, people asked me to create educational experiences with the information I'd used to shift my external life. Shyly, I agreed. A building I'd walked into years before for a yoga class and said, "I'm going to have an office in here one day," had a room up for subletting. The woman who rented it was a spiritual mentor in the community whose intuition urged her to call me.

This didn't excite me in excitement terms. I felt obligated to follow through as I'd promised to step into the plans that were spiritually aligned with God's plan for me and I hesitantly knew this was one of them.

I signed a lease, wrote a huge risky check with my income tax money, and got a custom made sign. Slowly and steadily, people came.

Whatever they asked of me, I designed. Workshops, expressive arts summer camps, sacred community circles and parenting classes unfolded. At the beginning of each, I regretted putting myself out there, sure I wasn't ready. Every time I expanded an inch, I'd contract a mile. Never with any boundary I set, uncharacteristic business decision I was guided to make, or in putting myself out there, did the sky collapse causing my ending, as I felt it would.

The only motivation I'd ever known came with an aim to *get out* of something. When there was nothing to get out of, I had no idea how to create. There was no top of a well in view to climb to. I was already out of the well, which wasn't motivating because the climb felt finished. I had no idea I could motivate myself with the option to get *into* what I wanted to get *into,* instead of only knowing motivation to get out of life's trap.

Cuddling on cold nights with my very-missed friend, *trust,* was my new motivation. Freeing myself from the mental cages I swore to get out of, I sometimes found myself slipping sideways, right back through the bars, to skirt out of the responsibility of showing up, in fullness, like I was being guided to. It's easy to hide in cages, and it's easier still to say you want to be seen, than actually letting yourself *be* seen. Carrying my broken pieces of my house of ego in my back pocket, I showed up anyway. *With,* my friend *trust.*

Fast forward.

Rebirth.

"Forgetfulness of your true nature is true death; remembrance of it is rebirth."

—*Ramana Maharshi*

I DIDN'T BELIEVE them. I wanted to feel it.

As we made it to the center of my suburban street on a gorgeous warm summer day, more of my waters leaked down my leg, sliding past my green summer dress as I held onto my partner through a contraction. My best friend used a towel to wipe up my legs. The same best friend that laid with me while Averiel crawled all over me while I fearfully sobbed about how I was going to pull off mothering two children a decade before. We stood in silence for a minute while a neighbor cleaning up dog shit in his yard watched us with a quiet smile.

It was a Tuesday afternoon when I decided to leave the comfort of my own home where I'd been contracting with short duration contractions every three minutes since 3:00 in the afternoon that Monday. That means twenty four hours of no sleep, and a lot of exhaustion.

My membranes were swept that Monday at 10:00 am and by 1:00 pm my contractions were strong but intermittent. I was 5 centimeters dilated at the time. By Tuesday morning, I was 6 centimeters dilated. I was sure as I stood in the street, it wouldn't be long until she showed her face earth side.

I'd never been in labor before. They told me I couldn't. Or, at the very least I shouldn't. I didn't believe them then either, but I also didn't trust my body then the way I'd grown to trust it.

A lifelong history of pain induced grand mal seizures didn't help. My seizures come from certain kinds of pain sending a message from my brain to my heart telling it to stop, so my heart abides, slows down and I seize like in the movies. I fall down, can't breathe, struggle to not swallow my tongue, piss myself, and by the grace of God, have always come back to consciousness.

The last time I seized, I was seventeen. I swore to myself as I lay lifeless hearing my mother slap me on the back screaming "Please don't die. Your father will kill me if you die. Please don't die when you're father isn't here," while I couldn't respond, couldn't move, but was screaming on the inside, "I'm ok, I'm here."

In her reality, I wasn't. It scared me enough to swear to make it the very last one.

For those few moments, I was in no way in control of my body. When I finally "came-to", I declared I was never doing it again. Ever.

My past is one trampled in mixed messages about *the* body, *my* body, *bodies in general*. In a lot of ways, my body never felt like my own. It felt like it was a spectacle, a target, anything but sacred matter. I was constantly trying to protect it from others, while simultaneously rejecting it from myself. It was nobody's if I could help it. Not even mine. I didn't share my body with many others, even in casual ways like letting *handshakes* be normal. But, I sure did use a lot of drugs to *get out* of it and I've learned we can't heal the body until we're *in* it.

The first time I'd gotten pregnant was a year after I declared I'd had my last seizure. Doctors took my seizures into serious consideration because I'd never experienced the pain of child birth and they understandably didn't believe that I wouldn't seize just because I declared I wouldn't a year after my last episode.

My body was so tired and I felt so betrayed by it back then. It was so much easier to have a man I didn't know, slice me open and rip me apart than for me to take any responsibility for the power I possess through it all. I was used to laying down and taking it, even though I was fighting silently in resistant rebellion. What we fight with, we are the keepers of and I didn't want my baby to be waging wars against myself with me in utero. Even in utero, they feel it all, and all of it, changes them.

Although there was talk of a vaginal birth after cesarean with my second baby, my doctors certainly didn't recommend it especially because placental rupture is more likely the closer a birth is to a previous cesarean. I didn't trust myself then, though I desperately resented that fact. I was mad at myself, and at my body, as I felt it was rejecting me, so I rejected it. The more I felt it demanded I surrender to its weakness, the more I fought it and the weaker it became.

My children's lives taught me to get right with my body. To be one with it the way I believe we are all one with the universe, with each other, and I am no exception to that rule. If I wasn't going to get right with it for my sake, I'd get right with it for theirs. My body wasn't rejecting me all of those years, it was communicating with me, but I was listening in resistance rather than compassion.

This pregnancy came eight and a half years after my last birth. I'd gone to the first OBGYN that my insurance suggested. The vibe felt the same as the doctors office of my childhood where my mother was told my seizures were tantrums. Intuitively, I knew that though they were saying they would *try* to honor my wishes, they wouldn't when it was down to the wire. I was sure they'd use scare tactic after scare tactic that again would make me question my body's ability *or my sanity*.

Consciously selective, enveloped in visions of natural child birth, I sought a feeling of safety in finding a doctor to believe in me, as much as I *wanted* to believe in myself.

Walking into her office all sorts of, "If you don't give me what I want, I will *accidentally* have this baby at home," I caught her attention. She was young, bold, and was as much of a professional rebel as I was. I could tell my demand challenged her to her liking. I assured her I could pull this natural child birth thing off. I told her there is no way I'd ever get an epidural because I hate needles and there was never, ever going to be an induction using pitocin. I know all about how those stories go down and I didn't want one of them to be mine. Authoring this birth experience into a check off the ole bucket list would require a ton of practice in mind over matter and soul-based intentionality.

She promised to give me what I want *within reason*.

The 32 week ultrasound showed that my baby was in a breech position which didn't change by 37 weeks. There was two ways out of this: a repeat cesarean or a procedure called a version which wasn't guaranteed to work. A *version* attempts to manually flip a breech baby from the outside of the womb. Everyone except my partner, including my doctor told me to go with the former and just get a cesarean. Especially, because one, versions are considered pretty painful, and two, even if it worked, she may flip back into a breech position anyway.

I went with the version. Though versions are often done with an epidural, I opted out in my attempts at being conscious, wanting to feel every last crawl space of myself.

The moment she was turned into proper position, I felt a difference in the way my body handled her.

For the first time during my whole pregnancy, I felt us working together. For months of sickness, I questioned whether this baby and I would be compatible at all in the outside world. When she became face down in utero, we flowed differently together.

We were one step closer, together, to getting the birth experience I desired for the both of us. Unmedicated, alert, and natural. That was the dream anyway.

After rejecting the hospitals attempts to place me in a wheelchair up to the maternity ward as I continued to stop through contractions in the hallways, I was told I'd gone from 6 centimeters to 8 centimeters in a few hours. It was 5:45 pm. Surely, it shouldn't be long.

My doctor had said that my upper waters had broken, but there was still a pouch of water between the baby's head and my cervix that she wanted to break. I stared at her with a clenched jaw, feeling my resistance to any manual interventions at all.

As if my subconscious heard my call, right then and there, more of my waters broke *on their own*.

Sinking into the Jacuzzi, I rested for over an hour at 8 centimeters dilated. Being in water slowed down my contractions remarkably. The second I got back on land, they came full force again. However, they were still short, intense, contractions close together. They were too short for doctors standards.

By 12:00 am, I was so exhausted I attempted with fail to sleep, meditating to relax in and out of consciousness. The contractions came with a different, deeper kind of intensity. I couldn't get comfortable through them. My instinct was to hang my arms over the back of the raised bed and get on my knees for the closest thing to comfort I could find.

The room was dark. My partner and friend were lounging, sleeping at times I'm sure, as the nurse sat next to me on a computer. Everyone else's inactivity was annoying as fuck.

I came to a blunt realization that no matter what, no one else can go through this *for* me. And even though they were there, they couldn't go through it *with* me.

I was exhausted and wanted relief. More than anything, I wanted to sleep. Somewhere between the hours of one and four am, I laid face down like an almost-dead-opossum roadkill and whimpered to my doctor, "I'm just so tired. Help me." Exhaustion is inexhaustible, itself. It is only for the human to contend. I'd given into it. Exhaustion was winning and I was ready to let it.

My contractions weren't long enough to get the baby out. We talked of pitocin which I refused, begging for anything that would make me feel better. She refused as long as she could. I stared at her demonically, pressuring her, "You're not listening to me! I need something! I can't do this!"

She was listening to me! She was just listening to the nine months she'd heard me say I'm going to pull this off. She wasn't up for hearing a different story now, in the heat of the moment.

The nurse kept saying, "You've made it this far! I'd never make it this far. I've seen natural births before and you're handling it better than most. You can do this."

Everyone's rejections of me feeling any relief with their cheerleading made me wanna kill them. They finally called the anesthesiologist and I sat in silent rage as I heard them explaining the risks of the procedure. I knew damn well at any given moment a contraction would jolt me away from a 20 minute attempt to stick an epidural in my spine. Being *heard* appeared to mean more to me than anything, as far as relief was concerned.

The anesthesiologist was on his way when more water worked its way out with each contraction. Time had stopped. I'd gone inward resisting hearing or seeing anyone's agitating faces or voices.

I never felt the need to push. From all I'd read, I was intent to let my body do its thing. My doctor told me to push through the contractions. I bore down through my first contraction of pushing, still with my arms hanging over the bed, holding myself up by my knees. I realized that I had a serious unconscious resistance to pushing, which was apparent in everything I'd done or not done in my life up until that point. So much fear came up around the notion of this being over, of giving in to my body. My own birth via my mother was traumatic energetically, set aside being pulled out by forceps because my mother was in-the-spirit-of-the-times, strapped to a bed, too numb from a spinal to push.

Birth is hands down, our first real trauma no matter how serene it is, but I do believe the energetic imprint sets the tone for the experiences we create for ourselves throughout life. I'd come into a world that scared me and wished I hadn't, and birth, no matter how we slice and dice it, is a death of the life we knew that came before it. Creating, birthing, I resisted the possibility of finally bringing me to my death. And it did. But, not how I'd expected it might.

The only times I'd ever surrendered my body the way it was being requiring during labor, was in the moments right before I'd have a seizure when everything smelled different, until complete stillness struck after a momentary relaxation. Surrender of body in this sense, meant unconsciousness. Space travel into the black for a hot minute.

"I'm going to have a seizure! I can't do this!" my fear barked at my doctor with my second push.

"There's only one way out of this, Stacy," she said with as much exhaustion and frustration as I was feeling myself. My resistance was apparent in the bags under her eyes. I'd try it her way, *for her.*

The anesthesiologist knocked on the door twenty minutes after his scheduled time. The nurse and my doctor glanced at each other and reluctantly said, "She's pushing!" and closed the door with him on the outside of it. I know they were taking a chance on those words. They wanted me to push, but I wasn't sure I was ready. They demanded I use my body the way I'd originally intended.

It's one thing to intend to do something, and a whole different ball game to do the something we intend. One requires breathing into possibility, the second, requires changing physical matter. Changing matter invites movements from the matter we change that are risky, and out of our control. I'd breathed for nine months and thirty six hours of labor the possibility of making this birth matter, but there was a risk in letting it move from me, into the outside world that I wasn't sure I was yet willing to take. Vulnerable like a victim, being asked to be pushy like a perpetrator, I was on the edge of my fears and they were headed straight from the place I'd kept them hidden in the dark the longest. My vagina, the birth place of my claim to creating all things in the world.

By my fourth push, my doctor told me to get in the shower.

I'd initially told her I love running water and would love to deliver my baby in the shower since the hospital has a no-water birth policy. The very second I got in the shower, on all fours, the water running down my back, I screamed, "She's coming!"

Right then and there was my first instinctual urge to push. I screamed like a lion roars. I screamed from the depth of my guts.

There's nothing I could've done to not let those sounds exit my body. My whole system moved together in sound, in spine, in power. I could never have separated one thing from another in that moment, but one thing I was sure of, what that the seat of my creative push didn't make me a perpetrator, and my vulnerability wasn't victimhood. I was uncomfortable on a tile shower cushion of my own aliveness.

I may have pushed four times tops in the shower. All I remember is putting my hand to my vagina, feeling her head and knowing what I had to do. Screaming, clenching the white tile on the walls, hearing my doctor say, "Her head is out, hold on," and then flipping to a seated position staring at black and blue knees, and exhaustedly holding my baby in my arms as the water ran across my face.

I was the first to hold my baby. Of three births, this was the first time this was true.

Someone helped me up as I walked from the shower to the bed with my placenta still inside. The after-birth happened when I was already holding my baby suckling on my breast like a warrior.

Our labor was essentially 36 hours long.

Every time a medical intervention was talked about, my subconscious got my body into gear and my body immediately responded with its own work. Attributing this to imprinting the memory of what I wanted, long before the memory came to fruition, my body gave me a reason to trust her when I got out of her way with the fear I'd held her captive in the cages of before now.

She heard my call and I let her answer.

It wasn't the four hour relaxed birth story I'd written. It was her birth. It was my birth. It was *our* birth.

Much like the story I was born into with my own parents, it wasn't written as I'd have hoped, but my parents and I have a story of us, and the outcome is prevalent in my life being fully lived. Because this is a love story after all, I love them for their characters in it.

In my commitment to not letting the story of my birth, be the same story I'm living into at my death, I've found that what we write in unconsciousness is arbitrary, but what we consciously live into, is everything.

My doctor believed me the day I walked into her door and handed her baggage that would've put any obstetrician on alert to know that they were taking a risk on their "professionalism" in a fear-ridden system by giving me the experience I wanted.

She believed in me then and she believed me in those hours that I didn't believe in myself, just like my seventh grade English teacher did.

I felt it all, just the way I wanted it. Thank God I didn't feed into all of the people who stared at me like I was stupid when I said that I wanted this birth experience to be a final rite of passage for myself in proving that I'm finally connected to my body, I finally trust my body, and I will never again reject the power that it holds for healing itself. I will never again get in the way of my own power, even when it hurts like hell. Her birth story, is more than a birth story to me.

It is my own rebirth. For the first time since my own infancy, I really trusted my body along with the world it lives in.

I didn't believe them, and thank God I didn't.

I often get called a warrior, for whatever reasons people decide to call other people such things. I didn't truly obtain *warrior* status until giving birth.

I'm not a warrior because I persevered pain. That, I've always done.

I'm not a warrior because I ripped myself wide open to bring life into this world.

I'm a warrior because I trusted. I trusted even when I was shitting myself *(literally)* to do so.

I'm a warrior because like the warrior with a bow and arrow, agile, running on a log across a river in bare feet, with grace...who trusts her feet and the ground beneath her, I trusted the process. I wasn't a pawn to the process, I was a creator in it, just like the warrior.

This was what my life had become. A continuously unfolding miracle I could depend on. The miracle of infinite trust for what is. What is, I'm certain, is that each push of ourselves into the world, feels like a tiny death, but not to our spirits, only to our egos attached to everything that came before it. An old version of us dies with every birth we're willing to give to something new in our lives. No longer would I be someone afraid to know myself on the other side of giving birth to something new. In fact, I'd invite it. Invitation is in itself, a short ceremony of giving birth to trust.

Rewriting The Narrative.

"There is greater agony than bearing an untold story inside you."

—Maya Angelou

I NEVER GOT to finish my life story, owning it, the first time I puked out my fears into words on a page in the bathroom. Writing was therapeutic, but rereading the piles of words that were the building blocks of what I knew of myself, made me want to knock them all down. My foundation was crooked and my insides dark. There was no love in my story.

I had a stark realization that my story was worth nothing, but commonality among all of the other people that led fucked up lives. It was an adventurous tale of "Oh, I've been there too, we can persevere the shit together," but life whispered other plans in my ear that day. It wanted me to write a new story. One of my own, that was written on blank pages of my own consciousness, not written as a response to all of the junk and projections life threw at me. I set off to create who I wanted to be considering who the highest version of myself, given the exact same circumstances, might show up in the world as. Becoming her became my *only* goal, and still is.

I wanted to know the me that never heard the words, "you're stupid," or "you'll never be able to do that."

After years of unraveling old stories, I became fully aware that this is the very beginning of my life story.

Life is either ending or beginning for us, daily, and we can tell which one we choose by which one we focus on.

Throughout the years of unlearning how to be in the grind, of setting boundaries of what no longer served me, or waking up feeling like I'd throw up from loneliness, feeling misunderstood, uncertain, impatient, and like a tantrum-ing child, I learned one very important lesson.

When we are spirit led, where there is a void, creation happens. We can be *in* the void, or *become* the void. If we are *in* the void, we can't find honest reprieve. Addictions are a pseudo-reprieve and only for a moment.

Addiction is merely resistance. We live in a society that provides sanctuaries for people to drench themselves in self forgiveness for 30 days (and call it rehab), for giving into their own resistance to actually show up to their potential all those years they wasted unsuccessfully, addicted to the chase of validating their self-worth.

The chase can be the sum of disruptive thoughts that keep us from our moments, the food we hate to love, or drugs, but when we're on the chase, we all have one very prominent feeling in common: we're unsatisfied and unrested though we satiate every want and rest more than we should, figuratively speaking.

All those years I spent addicted to external and internal stimuli, all I was chasing was the feeling that I have today.

Not so regrettably though, I ran down terribly unstable dark allies to find it.

Here's the thing about wrong turns, they're exceptionally easy to correct. We simply turn around. Sure it may take thirty more seconds than we'd like, but the opportunity to turn around when we know we're headed down the wrong road, means everything can be chosen again. It is not our detriment to have chosen "wrongly," it is our opportunity to witness where our feet land and choose again.

It's hard to hear yourself think when you're addicted to the game of what "everyone else thinks."

Tackling our own resistance and playing too long in the dark will be a practice to overcome while we're human. It's still an unrelenting bitch some days, to show up when I'm called, sit down when I'm asked, or be present when I should be "doing" something more. But, I believe the cure to all addiction that doesn't serve us, is harnessing the light, which can only come from our willingness to *be* it. Which in simplest form means, knowing ourselves in our grace, rather than our hell.

Instead of chasing our own demons in the dark, hoping to God our guardian angels follow us, we can choose to walk with our angels, rather than our devils. When we show up, not because we're not afraid, but because we know to not do so would be torturous to the soul, we can be assured we're choosing our angels. Our devils say we *must*. Our angels say we're *allowed*.

Giving up on our resistance to show up in truth, in spirit, in glory, is the foundation for healing any addiction, including the addiction to the stories we keep telling about our lives.

When we *are* the void, our *own* light funnels in to fill us.

Becoming void of who I'd turned into based on defenses toward a fucked up world, I'd fully let go of what no longer served me though my old scripts of oscillating between questioning whether I was the victim or the perpetrator didn't completely disappear. Though it continued to spin in my head on a regular basis, it began not to matter.

The constant search for what went *wrong*, ended.

Flashbacks from childhood, of my grandfather's touches, my mother's look when she was too far gone in her rage, my father's happy smile stirring at the stove, during the last beer that'd send him too far over the cliff for his aggression to stay at bay, had become images. Only images.

They came most often in the shower. I'd close my eyes, letting every earth-like, life-living molecule I prayed would know peace as a little girl, fall onto my eyelids and see old stories float into and away from my consciousness. That was all.

Old tendencies to chase down the memory, to feel it in my body as if it was happening right then, so I had someone else to point a finger at, as to why I couldn't be currently present to my life, were neutralized. The charge had subsided because I'd let it *move through me* instead of becoming a brick wall when it felt like the charge came *at* me.

Of anything I've ever trusted in my entire life, the only thing I never doubted was my connection to a creator. Though at points God felt like an absent father, the higher knowing in me knew he was right in the water I wanted to keep safe from universal demise. God pumped through the veins of my dead, abusive, pervert grandfather, and through the veins of mother Theresa. Of this, I was sure of.

God is in my mother's unshed tears and in the breeze blowing through a dress made by her, *hated and worn by me*, after a day I didn't get yelled at once. God is in the time between when my father's father asked if he could hold me on his death bed when I was eighteen months old, and me giving up the fantasy that if *only* my mother would've let him hold me in his vulnerability, I'd have known love, if only for a moment, but remember it for eternity, of someone I'd never know, but terribly miss. God is all of the spaces in between the images my body had physically and photographically held onto that made up a story that my mother was a cunt, my father was an adulterer, my grandfather was a pervert, my grandmother weak, and me, unlovable.

Allowing the images to flow through me like the water that washed over me when they came, freed me from having to keep up the chase.

I wasn't playing detective in my mind, in search for the missing pieces of myself that life stole each time it knocked me over. I was whole, and so were the people who perpetrated against me. I didn't have to let them into my world, one day longer, but I did know how to love them from the edge of my own boundaries, even when my boundaries said, "Stay the fuck out! Thank you. I love you. Now, out."

I hadn't been ready to let them off the hook for damning me into incompletion before. For raping me of my worth, robbing me of my will, and murdering the voice of a loving little girl who only wanted everyone to be happy. Before, I didn't know that me letting them off the hook, wasn't about giving to them. It was about giving to me. Forgiving somehow feels like getting.

The more I gave myself the freedom to let go of the old stories that had re-traumatized me on a daily basis for years, the ones I was always trying to run away from, the more I was aware that forgiving others was not my greatest feat. Forgiving *myself* was.

I didn't need to forgive myself for stealing cars, being the perceived druggie slut no *normal* parent wanted their kid around, or for the irrationality of my pregnancy escapades of throwing tables at my children's father. Those were all errors in perception at a time I didn't have the tools to trust that it was ok to love, despite what the world showed me. What I really needed to forgive myself for was my unwillingness to let go of the angst that I operated on up until that point. The angst of holding the world hostage for my own feelings of imprisonment. That's what my original story was about.

I was a prisoner in hell. Hell sucked. I would get out of hell. Insert a boring stick figure image here.

This is where the story of my life begins. I'm not a prisoner in the dark. I never was. My error was to believe in the same hell *they* believed in. A hell of the grind, the heart, the body, the earth. Hell was chaos and always a prison *for nothing*. I believed in hell more than I believed in the peace I prayed for on water droplets. When I asked to get out of hell, I didn't expect an answer, but if I did get one, I was sure the only way out of this hell was death. Death was my sanctuary, my refuge.

Every day, I worshipped death as my ticket home to God, was a day I regrettably missed living fully in the grace of God Itself.

Being spirit led, then heart led, doesn't make a damn thing *not* scary but it makes everything on the never ending journey of catching glimpses of heaven, everywhere we go, worth it.

Heaven was always there, smiling right at me, patiently waiting for me to give up my obsession with what's *wrong*, so I could finally relax into seeing, *what's right*. Right now.

There were never any great white sharks at the deep end of my aunt's in-ground pool, though I never went beyond four feet because I was certain they'd be there. Despite checking before I got in, and all signs pointing to there not being any sharks in the pool, I never swam in it without a sense of needing safety from sharks swimming at the other end of it. When no one was scaring me, no one was hurting me. When no one was there to judge me, I was scared, hurting and judging myself. Forgiving myself for exaggerating every *negative* experience and turning it into my *entire* experience was a brutally embarrassing fall to my knees.

The world is only giving, and we get to decide what it's giving for. I believed it was giving me hell. Now, I'm choosing to let it give me peace under the possibility that we get to choose what we want to take from the world. I had to forgive myself for damning all of those who damned me, into the same hell I swore I wanted out of, *and, for* not knowing sooner, that there was a way to release us *all* from it.

The doctors that made me doubt my motherhood were not the culprit, my *doubt* was. I no longer needed others to validate my paranormal sightings, or put an approval for sanity stamp on my past life experiences. I realized that my greatest enemy had been my fear nestling itself into my neurons. I dedicated to letting spirit move through me by quieting the loudest battle field I'd ever been on. The war of myself. Spirit couldn't do that until I gave up the fight.

Not through sitting in quiet places, but through engaging in life as a continuous meditation. As I am a mother, and life is my creator, it occurred to me that I could look at life the way I looked at my mother. Harsh, cold, brutal. Or, I could look to life, to mother me, the way I strive to nurture my own children. Life wanted to mother me. I wanted to let her. That looked like shutting up when I was redirected, receiving big hugs even after a stupid mistake, and trusting that no matter what, it absolutely has my best interest at heart. Ultimately, this led me to consider the same about my mother.

Images still passed through in visionary fashion, but my eyelids just rode the white water rivers of life's stories that pass through our shower faucet daily. The stories we don't consider ourselves a part of, that were pissed out by our ancestors into our today that we bathe with. The images came, but I remained at peace, and for once, I let them come without fear they would destroy me. For once, they'd come *and* I let them go.

Just when I'd truly given up on everything that'd ever defined me: friends, jobs, old relationships with my parents, old ways of thinking of myself, he showed up in my view. The split second I saw him, a strand of curled hair falling forward from his face as he lifted up his niece while I entered the room, I *knew* he'd be the father of my children.

Three years earlier, a friend called me who I hadn't spoken to in months. We ended the night in a large outdoor crowd of a band she insisted we go see. A man neighboring my dance moves smiled and asked, "Who are you married to in the band?" I laughed and said, "No one but I guess I was born to be a rock star's wife."

There he stood, the guitarist of that band. Of course, I didn't know that when I first met him.

Intuition is interesting because I do believe it knows what it knows and I also believe sometimes its timing can be radically far removed. I knew better than to force anything. I'd just let it be, seeing what came. After months of casual exchanges of love making and Breaking Bad marathons, we found ourselves in the greatest story ever written by me.

A Real Time Story.

SINCE I WAS a little girl, I spoke to God as if he was some foreign, unreachable man who my longings for, closely resembled my longings for my father. I knew he was there, but could rarely reach him, never giving up believing one day, that he'd come pick me up on his motorcycle and take me for ice cream, even though my mother told me he wouldn't.

I was a very good student for God, but a horrible student of people. My entire life, I saw right through people so much that I stopped trying to figure them out. I swore, I knew them. I held them hostage to being the person I believed they were. I didn't let them grow because I knew what they had done and what they had done was hurtful and something I didn't understand.

I was so caught on trying to understand why *they* could do what they did, I never dared create *my own* story in the matter. I was focused on theirs, so I could find *my* place in it. What I didn't realize is that ego is met with ego, and this is the place I saw right through them to *and from*.

I'd neglected my days of seeing right through to the heart in all things, somewhere in childhood, but I wanted them back.

The entire time I withheld my innate knowing that each and every one of them was just a whole world, a part of God, an ancient molecule, that once, I'd do anything to save from its forever doom. I wouldn't save it because it owed me anything, but because I honored its perfect right to be exactly and clearly, what it is. What it is, is alive and always beautiful from the right angle. What it is, may be like Arizona meteor showers that sometimes make you wait for it to show itself where you're standing, but it's there, and if we stay long enough we'll see it shine.

Really though, the layers I put between me and the world when I believed I was in the right to be angry, were the only things keeping me from *myself*. They weren't holding the world to their mistakes or teaching anything at all of value. They were holding *me* hostage to *my past*. Everywhere I went reminded me of an embarrassing mistake I'd made or was witness to. Both added layers between me and the intimacy I was able to share with the world.

When I realized God and people were the same, I became a faithful student to both. Not the masks we were all hiding behind. A good student of creation seeks God in everyone. I'd begun the practice of true sight.

My mother was my greatest muse, hands down. I don't know who I'd be if I was given a mother who sprinkled fairy dust on every boo boo and wiped my tears with a kiss. Like every other obstacle in my life, I judged as some injustice to my soul, I'm not sure I'd want to know who I'd be if she didn't teach me how to take the deepest breath imaginable, only to learn peace in the length of my exhale the next time she shoved my head under water.

She taught me everything I know. Compassion. Forgiveness. Who I didn't want to be. Who I did want to be. What not to say. When to set a boundary. That the body is temporary and ever changing and it's perfect exactly as it is. That looking good isn't worth killing yourself over and that independence isn't the ultimate goal to conquer, but interdependence is. Poor is a mindset, not a financial status. That intimacy is terrifying as fuck, but profoundly necessary for growth. She just taught me ass backwards, exactly as my life had progressed.

My formative years were my winter, and spring has come.

Spring didn't come when I forgave my mother or made excuses for my father. Spring came when I realized my mother, my father, and every single other person on the face of the earth that scared me, crossed me, resented me, or told me I was worthless, were not their actions, nor was I, their projections.

Spring came when I finally got back to my inner child's knowing that there is an entire life present in every fiber of all things. *That* life became the focal point of my vision rather than the zombified shields the *real world* was hiding inside of. That life, like a heartbeat, is a whispering signature for each living thing and I wanted to be quiet enough to hear it.

"Be the light" isn't reserved for *being*, it's reserved, first for finding. It's giving up the commitment to the anticipatory hunt and committing to the life force of the kill. It's being the essence and not the game. Orson Scott Card brilliantly says, "In the moment that I truly understand my enemy, understand him enough to defeat him, it is then that I also love him."

The love that pulsed somewhere deep in the veins of my perceived enemy wanted to experience itself through *my* witnessing of it. Like my parents, though blame was an easy deflection of taking responsibility of owning my authority, my greatest enemy had always been myself.

When I found the light in the dark spaces of my mother's teeth, the same ones that bit my ass so hard I couldn't sit down for an entire day, I could've likened her to the Virgin Mary. She is not a saint. She's not a prophet, but she is the mother I chose to teach me about sainthood and prophecies. Not a day in my life did she teach me the way I believed I wanted to learn, but teach me she did. Her greatest teaching came from the hidden gem she hides inside of herself that her own inner child is too ashamed to play with. By watching her, I learned we don't have to believe the stories we make up about ourselves if they hurt us.

My mother still longs for the boy she never had. She's still terrified of the fierceness of a wild, weird creature with a vagina she likely also didn't trust herself with that found a home in the world through a body she hated. One of her most consistent pieces of advice was "whether you love someone or you hate them, you still care about them." But, you cannot love something born, from something you hate, without *committing* to love. That was a step she'd missed in the parenting books she didn't read.

She still pines for her husband to see her as I longed for her to see me. She hasn't seen me once in my life. What she does see about me hurts her. She sees everything she is, and everything she's terrified to be, all rolled into one.

When she'd rip my hair out or brush it aggressively when I was a little girl, telling me it didn't hurt when I was the one determining the hurting, I used to tell her that when she was an old lady I'd rip her hair out and push her down the steps in her *old lady* wheelchair. I decided not to follow through with that promise. When she wakes up from dreaming in her own nightmare, I'll be there waiting to hold her hand and I trust the part of her that's busy dreaming will finally take mine without slapping it away.

"What are you so happy about?" is a question asked down upon by my family to whomever appears to be happy, as if there is nothing to be happy about. Truly, it's asked with ultimate condescension.

I'm happy to allow myself to be free to grow into a higher version of myself despite that the world wants me to play small to make themselves feel safe from their own fears about me or what I represent to them.

In my mother's case, I represent *love* which terrifies her. I represent the *anti-Christ* to fundamentalists that don't understand me. Equally terrifying. Neither, my burden to bear. Their definitions don't define me anymore. Mine do.

I still don't remember it all. I don't know what happened to me that made me repulsed by penises or reject my vagina. Pinpointing why I felt like a perpetrator and a victim, got herpes, HPV, and vulvar dysplasia after having three sexual partners, isn't ever the focus I want to begin my days with. I don't know why the sight of flies makes me cringe as if I'm being violated, or what happened after my grandfather's fingers rested on my thigh in his pickup.

What I do remember is an ancient language that whispers to me that the people who hurt me, are not the stories I'd written about them. They are divine, misfits, trying to make their way through the world with a different lens than I'd have wanted to see it through.

When I see them through the lens of their mistakes, I see the same world that they see, and that's the world I didn't want to be a part of.

Writing a new story about me, freed us all up to write a new story about each other. Together, we can create a new world, a new lineage, a new book ending.

The day I first purged my life, I wrote about everything I was carrying with me. I wasn't even present to my own life. I was present to my mother's fears, and my father's patterns. I projected that I couldn't do anything and I believed myself. I projected that my partners would have affairs, and they likely did.

Not once, did I see anyone in my life as they were on the day that I saw them. I had defenses for every kind of character I met on the streets. Men, I saw as mysterious mazes I wanted to play in, but only for fun because they were just a part of the man-hunt game I liked to play with myself in the dark. Women, I saw as fake and competitive who'd rip each other to shreds the moment they disapproved in the content of another. Life, I saw as bleak, unfair, and as something that if no one else would consider helping, I would be a savior for, but I fought the world I was claiming I'd save.

I didn't see a damn thing clearly. Not one. Yes, I forgave my mother for her abuses. Yes, I was compassionate for the mistakes of murderers, working on my compassion for molesters, and extended deep compassion to saints, and lovers for the bravery of their work. Yes, I was intellectually aware that not every man on the planet would be in constant search of something better than me. Still, I didn't *know* these truths. I only wanted to and a large part of me believed they were reserved for others.

The moment I gave birth to my daughter, I understood something I hadn't before. If I would've believed I lived in the same body I lived in years earlier, I'd never have gotten out of my body's way to give into the power of its innate wisdoms for birth. Translate this to every other thing in life. If I believe my mother, my father, my friends, my world, my lovers, are the same as they were years ago, even yesterday, I am withholding myself from the potential to truly get to know them, as they are today.

There is *no better gift we* could we give to ourselves than seeing it exactly as it is and experiencing peace in what we witness.

Together, We Remembered.

"Important encounters are planned by the souls long before the bodies see each other."

—*Paulo Coelho*

MY PREGNANCY WAS horrible. Hyperemesis is what they call it. Worst whiskey hang over you've ever had in your life, for seven months straight, is what it looks and feels like. I didn't particularly connect to the baby because I was so ill. When she began kicking, she'd kick me so hard I thought she might break something. My ego made it personal.

She kicked me so hard in a moment of relaxation, that without tension surrounding her movements, I stared at my belly and heard a silent breath come through me. "I'm happy to be in a body, Mommy. I'm happy to be back in a body!"

Her kick, for the first time, felt like a celebration, a communication that the baby I'd sent to be with my angels, to guide me to her father, was here, healthy, and ecstatic to incarnate with me again.

From that point on, I spoke to her differently. I told her loving things, rather than expressed irritation about my discomfort.

Mothers know. You know? We do. We can often tell the temperament of our unborn children, the voids in the emotions of our toddlers, the unspoken fears of our grade schoolers, the person behind the mask of our adolescents, and the *who* our children used to be, that we'll never get back when they become parents themselves.

I also believe that there are some mothers, so muddied up in their own junk that although they can tell the temperament of an unborn child, the voids of their toddlers, unspoken fears of grade schoolers, they are projecting their *own* incomplete parts onto their children, and their children aren't who they think they are at all.

Rather, their children become a *symbol for their fears* instead of an *alter for their love*. If I couldn't be a daughter who received this, I'd be a daughter who gave it. My parents won't be buried before I take the time to see the people behind the parents I assigned them as. I wanted to be for them, who I fought them to be for me.

My unborn daughter, and my life were solidifying a deeper work being done through me, in which, everything I was surrounded by, had become a conscious opportunity to be an alter for my love or a symbol for my fear. Her mission in spirit, felt like a *greater coming* for me, than just her alone.

Years of unconsciously choosing all symbols pointing to fear, my daughters coming, was asking me, as a mother, to heal in a way I'd previously been afraid to, for her sake. Her life was asking me to go beyond the law of attraction, beyond physical healing, or emotional self-improvement, to step into a seeing I'd abandoned around the time I realized not all kids were saving water droplet universes falling from the sides of their bath tub.

During her pregnancy, I got back in touch with the little girl I once knew. We saved some water droplet universes in stare gazes on my coast-of-Greece blue bathroom wall, during vomiting sessions. I mothered her intent to see the world beautifully, so I could mother the daughter I'd been hesitant to connect with, who was living under my heart, the way I myself, would've longed to have been raised.

Mothers are both fact, and metaphor. We do this with our children, and we do this in every relationship we have. Relationships with our homes, our appliances, our vehicles, our intentions, our coworkers, our friends, are all shaped by honest intuition, or exclusive to the ego. We are either extending love or projecting fear, but never do we, for a second, become free of the responsibility to know whether we're projecting or extending.

We are always creating a story. Always. Whether we're authoring it, feel like an extra in it, are the star, or the production manager, we are writing ourselves *into* it based on what we project *onto* it.

Motherhood, like Selfhood is a story of creation extending from our fear or our love and we are the creators of where and when our extensions land and what their landings mean. My new daughter's birth landed in our freedom and freedom can only come from one place. It's not money. It's not education. It's not success, though all of these things may be byproducts *of* freedom, freedom itself, is only born in love. This is what I'd remember to project onto our story for the entirety of our time together on earth.

Freedom, is love.

Who's Actually Crazy?

"But crazy people never think they're crazy. You're sane just by virtue of the question."

—Jacquelyn Frank

MY OWN MOTHER says I talk myself into believing this shit. Isn't that lovely?

Aren't we all? Aren't happy people creating happiness despite miserable circumstances while miserable people, find misery despite happy circumstances? Isn't it lovely that we get to choose what we want to see?

We can get out of our self-imposed prison cells of self-condemnation, where we see hate outside of our bars, and emptiness on the inside, simply by asking for the key to our cell, opening it with our bare hands and stepping out into a flower field we once believed was a field of mines.

Life has a way of guiding us to our questions when we ask for the right answers, but if we aren't asking, our old answers that likely don't serve us, are running the show. Our show doesn't just influence those we are conscious of, it influences us all.

A year after meeting my rock star boyfriend, I walked the beaches of Avalon just before dusk. As a therapist, people frequently asked me for my wisdoms and this day, in solace, I asked for God's.

"What message do you have for me today, God?"

I can still smell the way the air felt, how the sun glared, and the muffle of his voice as he ran to me. He was a stranger, maybe five years younger than me, with a sexy Jesus-archetype look about him.

"I know this sounds crazy, but God has a message for you…"

I laughed so hard, receiving his courage to share with me, and said, "I literally asked for you about thirty seconds ago." We collected hermit crabs and waxed poetics about his views of "the word," and though I'd just asked for him, secretly I was reluctant to receive his messages.

Which is similar to when I needed a new car, but couldn't afford even a shitty one, but needed a seven seater for our newly growing family and my friend who was moving to my bucket list dream vacation spot called me and asked if I wanted to buy her car. Which, is ironically the car that drove me five hours to meet my shaman for the first time almost a decade ago. It is also my dream car. With a thousand dollars less in my account than she was asking for it, I asked God if I should make the commitment regardless of the funds. Literally five blocks up the road after sending this sonar signal out into the universe, we passed a sign that said, "This is the message from God you've been waiting for." I committed to it. Within two weeks, I was driving my dream car which was the perfect size and timing.

Four months later, exactly a year after a majestic, totally present experience of frolicking with that stranger on the beaches of Avalon, I walked that same beach, except this time there was no one on it. No one on it but me, the baby I was about to give birth to and God.

As present as I was with the stranger, I walked on that beach, safe as ever, three hours from home, at the very beginning of my labor. Soaking it all in, to remember the peace of it always, I didn't rush to get home. I trusted the messages *all* of God's messages had taught me. Trust.

Ask and we *will* receive *if* we are *willing*. Willingness though, is a practice, much like trust.

The day I realized I'd blamed myself for a decade for someone else's suicide, I realized every other person that had come to me for healing, I felt responsible to play God for, as if I was the only person they had left in the world. I pitied them for their stories, rather than empowered them in their truth. Pity doesn't empower, it breeds notions of incompleteness, but pity I did because I was afraid if I spilled some truth, someone would die, and it'd be my fault.

The Stacy show took a turn at every profound story I'd bought into for every action and thought I ever entertained. At each turn, everyone I interacted with, including my houseplants and pets, were affected differently. Had I known not everyone would kill themselves when presented with a problem I wouldn't fix for them, I'd have been a much greater teacher, much sooner.

Everything changes everything. We get to decide how everything is going to *feel* when it changes. We can see the light in it, or we can swim in the dark of it, but in all things, both can be found. The one we seek is the one we will find. It doesn't matter if we think we *can*, it only matters that we *will* find what we want to believe in.

I was searching in the dark for a person to blame for my incompleteness, for my repressed memories, persistent illnesses, and fucked up thoughts, but I was the missing link. I was missing that I was complete, and no search for a target to my missing pieces was ever going to present me with anything more than I already was.

All I ever wanted the world to let me be, was exactly who I was. I didn't get that I didn't have to wait on the world, one more day of my life, to give me permission to be it. That's when I became it.

I stopped searching for why shit happened to me, who was crazy, and where I should run to escape it. *What* I was going to *be* about it became my priority. My head rarely served me well except for its majestic knack for escapism.

Still enough to greet my heart with the wonderment I previously greeted my incompletion with, I listened to where it guided me to go and it ended me up in the arms of my life partner, in a business I never expected, in an ever-changing, but currently slender body, with adventures in the brilliant and the mundane that the jaded me I became, would never have noticed.

My body, I was certain now, was the very best friend I'd had through it all. In all of my attempts to leave, she stayed, and loved me anyway. Like a pet, my body is an animal practiced in domestication. I've considered that animals don't experience what we call pain. They just feel what we call pain, moment by moment, until they're through it. Practicing letting the animal feel without all the ideas that feelings hurt at all, is the stuff of life. That's when we let ourselves experience what it actually feels like to be alive.

Had I not spilled my guts onto a page that year, I'd never have gotten clear about exactly how jaded I'd become. Ironically today, Jades are the only plants

I simply cannot keep alive. I was a different version of every person I wished I could change. My life needed a change of heart. I gave it the one my soul was asking for the world to give it. *Me.*

Play. That's what my heart wanted to experience for the first time since I was three. I never got to play without fear of who'd be slapping me for picking up a play thing that wasn't a toy I was allowed to have. My life was not based in the truth of my playfully free spirit, it was based in my rebellion of a world that forbid me to experience it safely. My seeming free spirit had only been a rebellion of the cage I wanted to break free from. True freedom touched me with soft edges when I released the fight against non-existent bars that I perceived held me into a jail I must escape through the walls from.

Give the heart what it wants, and apparently, it opens us to a freedom beyond the kind of freedom we begged for in all of our advances toward it and rebellion against it.

For years, every move I made, that felt like I was *getting away* with it being good, was simultaneous felt with a guilty feeling, awaiting when I was going to get into trouble for it. I played anyway. I said *no* to people instead of being a coward. I practiced only doing things that were a *"Fuck yes!"* and I only invited things into my life that felt like they aligned with who I wanted to be. When I was wrong, I gave myself permission to make a change instead of waiting for someone else to change. No longer would I wait for someone else to decide for me, where *my* life stood.

Forgiveness only means that I am free from the belief that we owe each other anything at all. That was always my go-to. Cry baby me, believing I owed the world everything because it let me come up for air every once in a while. I played with not owing anyone, and conjured up the strength to realize, despite all circumstances, no one owes me shit. After this paradigm sank into every fiber of my psyche, receiving anything at all feels like an energetic orgasm. It's all a cherry-on-top kind of blessing.

I wrote a story of my life once and I deeply didn't want the story I had written to be my legacy. It took me writing it, seeing it outside of myself, being radically honest about its contents to know that sad, pathetic story, would always keep me running in circles, opening doors that shouldn't be open for curiosity's sake, and vying for *someone else* to give me the answers to my insecurities, begging for life to take pity on me.

I wanted a mom to hold the little girl in me, close to her heart, a father who wanted to be with me as much as I wanted to spend time with him. I wanted to be taught how to do things right, not be punished for doing them wrong. I wanted a voice, to be seen for who I was, and to believe that I was enough. I wanted people to protect me from bullies and abusers and molesters. I wanted them to take away the pain of what it felt like to be me, trapped inside of a body that the people who were closest to me told me was my ugly enemy.

If I said I wanted anything as a child, I was frequently met with, "You always want, want, want. You're so ungrateful," so I stopped wanting anything at all but to *get out*. I didn't know I was allowed to want anything good.

I'd written my life story resenting that I was never going to be the girl who knew what it was like. I would never know what it was like to be built up, and told I was beautiful, to have a teacher, rather than a critic, to know boundaries, or that it wasn't actually cool to act pissed off and impatient when waiting in a long line at the grocery store. I was never going to get to go back and be taught by the world that I was enough. The world doesn't care about my feelings. I got that when I read my own words.

Paul Simon like, I worked on my rewrite.

The Art Of Being.

"Human evolution has two steps - from being somebody to being nobody; from being nobody to being everybody."

—*Sri Sri Ravi Shankar*

I AM A nobody. I will always be a nobody. For years, I resisted this, seeking approval from my mother to validate that I was a someone. She never gave it to me. In an ass backwards way, I'm grateful she didn't. One day, I'll die and my ashes will dissolve in ancient waters to be drank up and pissed out by our predecessors. That takes the edge off. Likely, we'll all end up being a nobody. We may know Rumi's heart songs or Einstein's equations. Indeed, we do not know *them*. They will always be a nobody if we take away all of the labels our egos feel suited to wrap around their names.

Being a nobody, freed me up to become somebody to myself. The somebody I always wanted to have in my life.

I may never know what it's like to *have* all of the things I wanted for the hurting little girl that stares wide eyed at the world living in my heart, but I set out to *become* all of the things I wanted *for* her.

I believe my children when they tell me they see things that I can't. I give students a voice who are too *stressed* to learn, *not too stupid*. I hug people despite years of having to overcome my fear of letting people touch me intimately. I hug them close. I let it be real, and I stay with people, meeting them where they are. I create experiences for others that I wished the world would've provided for the lost girl inside of me.

The world didn't gift me its love in plain sight very readily. It didn't open my eyes to transcendental love or make me feel safe in the womb of mother earth. It just didn't.

I got really right with that. I knew it wouldn't. So, I set out to be that love myself.

The point in these words, like any nobody writing anything, is basically nothing.

What's in between these words is where healing happens. It's the moments in between when my mother told me I was fat, and I puked until my eye sockets turned blue, hated her, forgave her, then averted my eyes to the alter of my own healing, that shape the story of what my legacy will become. It's in my willingness to every day, let the battle of temptation that my mind wanders down in the avenues of its hell, be what they are, and see heaven anyway.

When life throws curve balls at me, I will take them *through* instead of *in*, so the balls do not become my story, but my dance moves, swaying around them, *do*. My legacy will be my slow dance with creation, and not the balls that tried to stop me from engaging in the dance.

I used to have a tattoo of Salvador Dali's clock with the time I was born, and clouds passing through to symbolize time as an illusion. Technically, I still have it, it's just covered up by something new, so only me and it, know it's underneath. Intellectually, I always bought into this concept but I didn't feel it in my bones the way I do now.

My mother is not *always* hitting me. My father is not *always* choosing other women over me. My peers aren't *always* bullying me. What stuck, stuck because it changed me. It changed me *only* in the beliefs about myself and I believed the beliefs I made. Trauma changes us, but we're bigger than our trauma. This I know for certain. We can set out to change our trauma just as it changed us. Setting out to change our trauma is the first tool I've found that cannot be used as a weapon against ourselves and it's the greatest asset we can give to our children.

My parents did the best they could with the beliefs they were indoctrinated to believe about the world. They were walking symptoms of soul wounds that by conception, could be called *post-traumatic stress disorder*, looking for a Band-Aid, not knowing, they themselves, *were* the cure. Like most of us, they didn't know they could change their beliefs and the whole world would cater on their behalf to whatever their new belief was. Their greatest asset *and* their greatest enemy was always themselves.

I believe in past lives and holistic living and I am surrounded by a world that values the same things. Others believe in fast cars, and beef jerky from dive gas stations, and they are surrounded by a world that values cars and jerky.

We get to pick what we believe, despite the advances of the world to pressure hose our doubts into submission to play small. What we believe will create our heaven, or our hell, here on earth.

The world told me I couldn't, and until I got a referral to an oncologist, I believed them, never even considering that I shouldn't (believe them). I couldn't get good grades, do it on my own, heal myself, find a partner, own a business, give natural child birth, be completely myself. The world told me I'd always have to fit in or I'd be kicked out.

I quit that world, and hired a new one.

That was an option my parents never told me about. They didn't know we were allowed.

Shit, I didn't even know I was allowed to like someone who didn't like me. I thought I had to judge them for judging me, thus we were both in my measly little prison. Others were *creating*, and I was resentfully *following*.

I didn't know the night I was old enough to realize, that I'd told my father I loved him right before bed every single night, not remembering him once ever saying it back, meant I could keep telling him, despite him feeling uncomfortable or not saying it back.

Leading with love, was for the weak. *Following* with resentment, was how the strong survive. Fuck that. A heart ripped open wide is the lover and leader of the bravest of souls who walk the earth and I wanted to become one of them.

The option of creating beliefs that made me feel good without someone else's approval never even crossed my mind. Considering maybe someone is having a really bad day, letting their behavior have nothing to do with my worth was not previously an option that was present.

I wanted someone to prove to me that they got the depths of the human condition that make us want to rip all of our skin off and bleed out on the floor because it fucking hurts. They had to get it *and* show me that there was another way to see this shit show. I wanted someone to show me flowers where I saw scars. The sight of one tiny flower growing out of a crack in the side of someone's brick house. I needed that.

So here's that flower sticking out of the cracks, sharing with you that it doesn't only get better, it gets fabulous.

I Used To Think Happy People Didn't Know Shit About Life.

"A riot is the language of the unheard."

—Martin Luther King, Jr.

I SPENT YEARS screaming at the world with keen insights to how it would be better if only *it* changed this way, or that way on my behalf. If only I was rich I could get away. If only I had a mother that loved me, I wouldn't be so resistant. If only I had a father who didn't burden me with his secrets, I wouldn't feel responsible for the weight of the world's emotions. If my parents weren't miserable in their relationship, I wouldn't fully well chase emotionally unavailable people to avoid my own fears of intimacy. The world won't change for us, until we change *for ourselves.*

Once I realized there was no problems to solve, I was free enough to create. My entire life was spent resisting a problem that felt like it never existed in the first place when I realized it was all taken care of. None of the problems I'd deemed as problems were actually standing in the way of me and my receptive-to-joy self.

My main problem was my belief that everything that challenged me to grow was a *problem* to be solved, rather than an *opportunity* to know myself in a higher way.

My resistance to surrendering decades of self-work, giving up everything I'd known for the sake of happiness, appeared just as uncertain as swimming in the shit of my sorrows had been.

I sent this to a publisher:

I used to think happy people didn't know shit about life.

I used to day dream about throat punching the happy girls in high school as I visualized them going to bed at night without train wreck thoughts and sleeping with dreams of Strawberry Shortcake.

I found them boring and I found boring annoying.

Obviously, if they were happy, they weren't paying attention.

As much as I may have said I wanted happiness, I never wanted *it* more than the identity that *I had persevered a bunch of bull shit.*

I wanted to let my unhappy-people-tribe know I got them and that I see what they see, and it's dark, and dirty, and there's filth in this world that those stupid happy people must not have had to go through. But we, we *know* the dark and we have each other to swim in it with.

Therefore, happy people were stupid because they didn't know shit about *real life.*

I definitely didn't want to be stupid. So, I didn't want to be happy.

I swear, I imagined their brains to look like a single goldfish swimming in a fish bowl without any decorations.

Just the bowl, the water, and the fish.

No emotions, no thoughts, just there, unpoetic in its deeply poetic simplicity.

They weren't real to me. My real, was pretty painful. I only trusted people that knew my kind of angst. I only trusted them because I believed we understood that it was probably a bad idea to trust anything at all. What we trusted about each other was nothing more than our common mistrust for the world.

It never crossed my mind that happy people worked with the same angst *my* people had, to *become* happy. Or that they too, may be persevering some serious bull shit just to *stay* happy.

Then came the *bridge to happy.*

The part when happiness appealed to me, not because I thought those happy people were any less stupid, but because sometimes I'd dance naked in my kitchen and I'd feel what happy felt like. I thought if I could be it, and stay smart about *real life*, it might not be so bad to devote my life to becoming it.

The *bridge*, is one that I built as I walked across it. Before I put that last piece down to safely take me to the other side of *happy*, I stared and bitched and complained at my destination.

I didn't put it down. I sat on my knees and held it intensely with a locked jaw silently stink-eying, "*Look Happy! Look at all the shit I did for you! What are you gonna do for me?!*"

I'd worked my ass off to built that bridge. I'd also worked my ass off swimming in circles of my unhappy *(only to end up thinking floating would be much easier than treading water to nowhere for the rest of my life)*.

I knew how to work my ass off; I didn't know how to *be* happy.

As I clung to that last piece on my bridge to happy, staring down the side of happiness, all of the fish bowl brains I'd gotten excited about throat punching for the *very* thing I was about to give up all of my hard work for, were fresh on my mind.

Happiness didn't respond. I sat with that last piece, holding so tight to the identity I'd gathered resources around, knowing if I laid it down and walked over it, I'd never be the same again.

I bucked at happy. I kicked the bridge I'd worked my ass off to build and sincerely thought about burning it down. If I gave over this last piece of myself as I had known me, what have I got?

Nothing.

I'd have no story. Exposed. A sacredly self accepted nobody, I'd have nothing more to work my ass off for and if I wasn't working my ass off, who would I be?

I'd be a fish in the fish bowl. Boring.

I'd been a lot of things in my life, but a simple minded goldfish swimming in a fish bowl was definitely not one of them. Or, actually maybe it was and I just couldn't see it yet.

That last piece didn't go down gently. I slammed it down and screamed, "*Take me bitch! I wanna know you so be worth this damn bridge and giving up everything I made for you!*" Happiness carried me into her wilderness. I didn't even have to take the last step. She carried me exactly where *we* wanted me.

Sometimes, I do feel like a fish bowl brain. Looking back on it, I was always living in a fish bowl, my water was just filled with a bunch of shit. This water isn't littered with train wreck thoughts, or trauma after trauma. It's clear.

I'd considered I was giving up on belonging to all of the people I wanted to help by letting them know, I *got* it. I got that the world is full of shit. And, I definitely didn't want to be in a tribe of fish bowl brains that dream of Strawberry Shortcake that shit heads like the old me thought were dumb and naive.

I was worried I'd forget everything I'd learned from the bull shit and never *get it* again.

Apparently, goldfish have no memory, but I do. I may not remember details, but I remember what it feels like.

The fact is, I don't forget. I don't forget what it was like swimming in the shit, I just don't have to swim in it anymore. The fact is, letting people know I *get it* isn't enough to help them at all. It was only enough to help *me* to know that they knew I did (*get it*). It was only enough to keep *us* in the shit we *got*. By all means, that shit sucks.

It's hard to put down that last piece on the bridge we build to happy. It's hard to not know who we're going to be when we step onto the side of *happy*. It's hard to think about disappointing the people who *get* it the way we *got* it. It's hard to surrender to not having a story to overcome.

When we're constantly *overcoming*, we leave no space for *our becoming*.

It's hard to give into a float when we've only known treading endlessly to nowhere.

I'll tell you what's not hard.

Happy.

Put down the last pieces on the bridge you worked your ass off building to get to her.

Go to her.

She'll teach you how to float.

An editor wrote me saying, "You're missing the most important part. Share with people *how* you became happy."

Believe In What, Not How.

"A bird sitting on a tree is never afraid of the branch breaking because her trust is not on the branch but on it's own wings."

—Unknown

I WISH I would be able to share with the world exactly *how* to become more of themselves, as I've found my happiness lies in shameless authenticity. Sure, I've been gifted paradigms and insights for shifts that I can share, but that's for a different book, and all of them will be obsolete if not for a faithful belief in healing.

I wish there was one mode of *how* that worked for everyone, but only a fool thinks their way is *the* way. When my boss said to me on my house search, "Whatever you want in life Stacy, focus on the *what*, not the *how*," I expanded my thoughts to let that statement be a metaphor for all that I did.

The world teaches us a paradigm of cause, so much so, that we lose sight of the effects we're causing by staring at the cause instead of the effect that likely, hasn't happened yet. I frequented the internal conversation of "what" my intention was rather than *how* I'd see it manifest, every day since he spoke those words. The method has *never* let me down.

To dissect how it happens is pointless because my how is still unfolding and will be different from anyone else's how. All I'm certain of is that one day, I realized there was nothing at all I wanted on earth a quarter as much as I wanted to heal. If it took me believing in the unseen, giving up junk food which at times felt like my best frienemy, leaving my job, or the country, I committed to heal.

Other people wanted houses or cars or to move out of their hometown at eighteen. I wanted to know peace more than I wanted any physical possession. I am certain that like every wise book tells us, the universe will conspire when we want something. I am certain that that doesn't simply happen by *believing*, but by *surrendering* everything we thought we knew yesterday to provide life an opening to let our dreams find us.

Healing became more important to me than any job, relationship, house, earthly security, travel adventures, education or socioeconomic status. In return, healing gave of itself all of the things I could've ever thought to want.

Both feet in, I didn't waiver from my commitment to heal. I drank everything in life in, the good, the bad, the bull shit, the profound, and committed to letting it heal me even if it felt like it was slicing me open with a butcher knife without any anesthesia. Which happened often *until* the masochist, the martyr and the pessimist of my childhood that taught me to believe it had to hurt to heal, took a back seat.

How we get anywhere on this journey is obsolete. It only matters that we want to be there.

I wanted to feel like I had a home. Not for fleeting minutes of safety-hood, but a log cabin in the woods, fire pit by snowfall kind of sturdy home. I knew I'd never find it anywhere on earth in any one place, person or possession. So, I went there.

I walked myself home to peace with the help of every intuitive nudge that I trusted more than I doubted. It kissed my face, smiling in awe at how trusting I'd become to its presence. It was the first thing that ever thought I was cute. That's how I knew I was home. The present me, no longer had a story that it wasn't safe to play.

We don't fulfill any mundane tasks. What we do, we do *to* and *for* us all. What we drink, eat, think, moves up and down the threads of our oneness and changes what was, for something *(ideally)* higher. We heal them all, when we heal ourselves. Our great grandparents, our great grandchildren and every shackled soul we ever longed to show the light becomes free in colorful doses, when we do.

Years, I spent waiting for the world to show me what I myself, wanted to become.

In my assertions to understanding what the cosmic connection between my star-crossed lover and I was, I wrote down a list of what I loved about him. I realized everything he was, I wanted *to be*. Most of it, I already was, I just never allowed myself to honor it fully in myself. He taught me to become, rather than sit around and wait for his ass to *be coming* home to me. His purpose in my life wasn't for him to be coming, it was for my own becoming.

I set out to become everything I'd always wanted on the inside. When I did, the world matched me with everything I wanted on the outside. I let him go when I became all of the pieces of myself I found hidden in him.

Healing Happens.

"Why are you knocking at every other door? Go, knock at the door of your own heart."

—*Rumi*

OUR GREATEST WORK is not *in* our work, but who we show up to our work *as*. We are naive to think that our greatest work is not to heal. In a society that its life pulse depends on sickness, the signs are everywhere. Healing will be our first, and our last work, in all of our work. If we don't first choose it, it'll choose us. It'll give us something to heal from.

The flip side of this is when healing is the priority, it also teaches us not to work. It teaches us to let it all be, exactly as it is, right now, in this exact moment, in every moment.

We even work to hold our stories. I worked harder to hate my mother than to love her. All I ever wanted was to love her. I hated her because she wouldn't let me. I held a noose tight around the neck of people that spread rumors about me and my grip didn't loosened after years of their absence, but it was strangling me. That's stifling to the countless ways I could use the energy of my hands, which are an extension of my desperate, pulsating, giant heart.

Whether we trust God or not, God is always present for the taking, keeping us so safe that we, without any rationally calculated reason, miraculously made it alive, to this moment now.

When I let go of every story that bound me and everyone I knew, to a burning hell of a past, my body transformed to a much smaller version than it had been since my vomiting and pill head, high school days.

When I make love to my partner these days, I share myself. I don't *give* me away in resentful feelings of violation. I make love to myself (with him), *not to him*.

I've learned that the best, most intimate kind of lovemaking is when we're sharing all of ourselves with only ourselves. When we do this, we let whatever happens happen, no matter who witnesses us and here is where we open doors to the transcendence of oneness.

I held back my affections because the affections I wanted to give, were scolded and my wants were annoying. I withheld who I was for the sake of catering to everyone else's fears. I thought that's what I had to do to keep *them* safe and me, *liked*. I cared more about what the world thought about me, than what I thought about it, so I hid myself for the sake of the world, damning myself to hell contingent upon their approval. I never had to, from day one, but from day one, I blamed them for making me. A form of self-torture we unknowingly commit to, is our relationship with insisting we damn those who damn us.

I made up a story about the story of my life. I believed that story. It's all perfectly true and everybody's got one. I'm not crazy, I suppose. Neither is my mother.

She challenged me at every turn, about every direction my life of healing took. The only thing that got in the way of us, was my belief that I had to believe her, or *change* her. The moment I had a doctor accept the lifestyle I'd chosen for my children, I stopped feeling crazy. Seeing my father's connection to me in previous lives opened me to love him differently. The only obstacle I ever faced in my life, was my internal war between *faith* and *doubt*. Everything in my life was only a symbol for one or the other. It wasn't until my faith swelled greater than my doubt that I was able to write a story I wasn't ashamed of.

What makes our stories is what we believe about them. I no longer wanted to believe in a story that didn't *believe in me*, so I changed my story from the inside out.

Right now, we are in charge of a mere memory that gets imprinted in time and space, literally. Our charge is creative intelligence and we use it to search in the void or to feel the fullness of the light.

William Blake says *eternity is in love with the productions of time*, but I wasn't for a majority of my life. Minefields of battle were my imprint and would be the imprint for my children if I didn't *stop* time, and *own* my space.

The real me, the one I hid when *once upon a time* the world made me believe it wasn't safe to play, wanted to own the actual space she took up, that she was once afraid to step into to create *new* things. It didn't matter if I was *too much* or *not enough*. I only wanted to explore my center and all of my edges. New feelings, experiences, and potential points of view with a heavy duty magnifying glass is what I was after. I was used to the same anger, annoyance, resentment, and victimhood. Every neuro-pathway had worked its way into a train track with very easy access to the door that unleashed my deepest fears, but I'd interrupted the tracks by derailing those fuckers.

My imprint was destined to be one vibrating from the frequency of neural-train tracks that led right to my freedom and I'd will anything to forge them. Because life is a mirror, I'd see myself in every person I met, who'd see *their freedom* in me.

There's a scene in the movie, the Golden Compass, where the characters are having what appears to be like-a spirit animal that follows them everywhere. Each character is followed by a different animal. When the human characters talked politely to each other in a passive dispute, their animals brawled wildly on the floor while their character composed a *proper* demeanor, saving face, masking their actual feelings. I'd always envisioned that this is what goes on between souls while we mask ourselves behind our niceties, our apprehensions and our small minded competition. Our souls play off of each other like an organ in a cave, echoing different tones in different crevices, but coming from the same original sound.

Lions circling each other. At every introduction that's what I envisioned in my hell days, waiting to see who was going to pounce first.

Tail-pointed-up cats. That's what my soul wanted to experience every time it encountered anything that could be considered a noun. I'd love it like stuffed animals in stores, keep it safe, and expect it to be friendly. Don't get me wrong, the soul is a verb, rever*berating, through the activity of an infinite amount of other verbs dressed in flesh. We're invited to let our soul do her thing which in the productions of time, turns the creations we nurture, into nouns, adjectives, more verbs and everything in between.

The only thing in my life that's stopped me from anything was merely my resistance to letting my soul call the shots because I thought my fear was more powerful than my spirit. I was wrong. Logic, always, always, always, had me shooting in the dark. Soul is relentlessly holding the light on my path in the roughest of elements and terrain.

We can hide *in* our souls, but we can't hide *from* them. When we think we are, they're still feeling it all, connecting to our lust for feeling alive even when we feel most dead. Our souls are having an experience our minds miss. They want to find more of themselves out while they're here. Anew. Inviting us to rewrite history by creating the future we want in the present. Presence in every way, is a production of the future and we are the film producers.

The memories we leave behind don't die at the end of a story or a life. They live on in the water-filled toilets we piss into daily, into our children, great grandchildren, and bleed into the collective unconscious of species we've yet to discover. If we never create a damn thing in life, one thing is for certain about our creations: we are relentlessly creating memories.

How does it feel to be you, all powerful, maker of memories, in charge of your next step, reading this exactly where you are, wearing what you are, being who you're about to become?

Each moment is a practice of being a *capturer*, not the captured. By capturer, I mean, a memory-making photographer, witness to the *truth* we've hidden from ourselves. The truth is, we are much, much larger than our stories.

Capital T Truth Only Finds More Of Itself Out.

"Other people will call me a rebel but I just feel like I'm living my life and doing what I want to do. Sometime people call that rebellion, especially when you're a woman."

—Joan Jett

PEOPLE WILL CALL me delusional. Doctors have told me I must never have had herpes. Skeptics will discredit the shamanic experiences I've had that led me *(along with psychedelic experiences)* to my own interpretation of blissful universal oneness. The very experiences that led me to heal will be doubted by outsiders and cherished by insiders.

No matter how much I've grown, I'll always be seen by those looking through their stained up lenses of all of their own yesterdays, who make me a perpetrator for their own desires for self-defense. I'm cool with that.

I don't have to believe what they see about me or about the world. My intent is to see a new person, in each moment. In letting them grow, as I always wished I was allowed to grow, without having my wings clipped every time I spoke of learning to fly, I freed myself to not be bound to every story I'd previously written about the world and the people in it.

I set out to *give* everything I've got, but never let anyone *take* a thing from me again.

My mother will still assert that I talk myself into believing what I want to. Hence, why anyone who ever healed themselves of anything *(and there are many*

164

of us on the planet) all had one fundamental thing in common. Withstanding the pressure washer force of doubt that life sprayed on us, *we believed in our healing.*

I hear a lot of rags to riches stories. They're intriguing and everybody who isn't bored or miserable in their own lives, will likely find inspiration in them.

I grew up with a mom that looked like Betty Crocker, who handmade my clothes, dressed me like her Barbie doll and treated me like *mommy dearest.* Riches looked easy, but came at a cost much greater than materials. My parents always made sure we dressed the riches part.

It was our insides, ripped up like rags that I wanted to sew back together. I wanted rags in heaven more than I wanted riches in hell, but peace taught me that there are no rags in heaven.

Only riches.

Hell, is whatever we make of it which always adds up to nothing. It's a maze of one big mind fuck, stuck on enemy territory.

People will say what they will. They may use these words against me and discredit my experiences, say I'm too arrogant, too catered to, because my experiences were likely better off than others who share their stories. But the truth only finds more of itself out and *this* truth is rightfully mine.

People will let their triggers define my stories and my words as worthy or not, but the thoughts of others do not define *me* anymore, they define *them.*

You're invited to believe in *your* healing. Believe in whatever journey you are called to in times of a need to heal and get out of your own way with doubt. Healing may guide you to a beer on a beach, a half climbed mountain, or a million dollars, but God is the design that will not lead us astray if our intent is truly to heal.

Healing happens when we believe in it, not when we wait for it to prove to us that it happens. It's not one of those, first I will see proof and then-I-will-believe-in-you situations. It's something to practice, letting life unfold within us, what it wants us to preach. Whether it's acupuncture, nutrition, spirituality, art, creating a life filled with extraordinary experiences in the mundane, whatever feels like a healing room to your soul *(and your nervous system)* believe in it and let it take you where it wants to go.

Learning doesn't have to hurt. We don't need to get slapped, or kicked when we're down to prove our resilience as I'd previously believed. The very fact that

I've gotten through three decades, and these words have found their way to you, through *your* decades, proves how very resilient *we all* are. We don't get away with not living. Life either lives us, or we live it.

It is in the choice to come alive *in* it, that we find it not only bearable to live, but extraordinary.

By natural order, each year of life, rips a layer of us off that kept us further away from the us we were once afraid to be. Each year, we get closer to the core wisdoms present in each of us, hidden under layers of mistrust, motives, and insecurity. By nature, we'll live into the 20/40/60 rule my star cross lover taught me, whether we try to or not.

Scrubbing my legs with clay from the riverbed, immersed from the waist down in cool, stream water on a sunny summer day, my star cross lover planted a seed in me that I wanted to sprout much sooner than later. I had released him along with all of the other stories I'd written about how it should be, of unrequited love, and who we were supposed to be together, but one story we wrote, was a story that changed everything about the direction of my book.

At twenty four years old, his words *(which were not his own)*, "When you're in your twenties, you care what everyone thinks about you. When you're in your forties, you don't give a shit what anyone thinks about you. And, when you're in sixties, you realize no one was ever fucking thinking about you in the first place," set me on a mission to be a person *willing*, and wise enough to live a life realizing, not only is it likely no one is thinking about me now, but that being a nobody, is the first place to look for the freedom I always sought.

If we never do any work at all, there is a potential to end our lives fully realized. I wanted to know what living that wisdom was like, *now*. To rip off the gauze that stood between me, and the inner world I left behind in childhood for fear the world might trample on what was left of me if I didn't hide it. There's always so much more to realize.

I get that I will never comprehend with words the profundity of full realization in human form.

As a psychotherapist and writer, it's an interesting dissonance to know that the most essential components for healing, cannot be put into words. Most of them cannot even be talked about.

No longer tallying up what the world owes me, or I owe it, with a belief that neither of us deserve the other, me the world, or the world me, a new story of my life is only now just beginning.

It feels clean, and trusting. In this story, I taste the food I chew. I smell the books I'm reading. I practice safe touch. I apologize without thinking I should kill myself. I don't forfeit my intuition just because someone has letters behind their name. Here, the dress my mother made me, came from loving me the best way she knew how.

In this story, I write my way into a life that would make my first fan, the lady who took away my writings in in-school suspension, proud.

I wrote it for me, knowing, I am the world, just like every other person, plant, or thing, I find myself in relation to. I wrote it simply because I exist and existence is power.

Elizabeth Gilbert perfectly summed up my life by saying something along the lines of the fact that if she wasn't creating something with her life, she was likely destroying it. My life found grace when I began to channel my power of existence on the side of creation, rather than destruction. Destruction is an alluring bitch who tells me sharks are in the pool when they aren't. She's the sister who locks you in the garage with no way of getting out and runs away while you're pounding on the doors.

Creation is my first mother. Quiet, stern, loving, all knowing. She teaches that it takes just as much energy to destroy yourself as it does to create yourself. Creation feels like a sensual hug, despite our intimacy issues.

I'd always dreamed of showing my father the redwoods. I knew he'd love them as much as I did. It gave me chills for years to think of us enjoying the majesty of one thing we could both connect on. Until, we did it.

It was then that I decided I didn't have time for sleep while I was dreaming.

It was then that I understood how incredibly true it is that we can't think our way into a new kind of living. We must *live* our way into a new kind of *thinking.* We cannot hold onto the fear our elders grew by, so like the song, I decided to teach my parents well. Much like their daughter, *resistant and brave*, they are letting me show them what I could never tell them, but not without a fight.

A Message For My Mother.

"I believe in love at first sight because I've been loving my mother since I opened my eyes."

—Unknown

OF ALL OF the shit my mother says I talk myself into, there's just one thing I wish she'd let herself believe in. It'd be the equivalent of seeing my father experience the redwoods. It's something she taught me by pissing me off enough to want to gut myself with words after twenty three years of resentment and distain toward life.

Here's where my words find their way to you, because <u>existence itself</u>, is <u>power</u>.

Now is when I become the woman I always wanted to have in my life, for someone else. Ideally, that someone is you because even if my mother *gets* it, she'll likely never relent from her desire to not give into me. Learning new information does not mean we've been wrong, or even misguided by the old. Knowledge is a stimulus package for soul economy, but she doesn't trust the economy.

She's too proud to give up the identity she's created for herself. Dare she admit to having it wrong, for she'd then have to correct herself. *Giving it up, admitting there might be another way,* would, in her mind, be defeat. Not salvation. Doing exactly that, is where I found my own salvation.

I recently overheard her say to someone with her hand over her mouth, "I've read her writings and she actually blows me away, but I would never tell her that."

Every word you've just read is dedicated to the little girl that lives inside of my mother who was too afraid to come out and play in the world that hurt her more times than she could stomach. Hurt was all she knew, so it was all she knew how to teach. I've come to show her differently, but she'll only *see* what I have to say. She won't *listen*. If there's one thing I can offer that little girl inside of my mother, or any other soul who wants change but is wading in fear rather than floating on love, it's the following message:

> We are verbs. Authors. We're authoring a continuous verb we call life but we are the verb behind the authorship. We can be alive or we can be liv-*ing*.

We either consciously write, or allow our lives to be written by believing bullshit someone wrote about us. Distracting ourselves with the stories of others and investigating how they will choose to fit into our stories is time robbery. Literally.

When reading good books, we hand our imagination over to the author.

We're busy trying to find clues about what the other life authors in our lives are scribing:

> *"He said he loves me but he can't be with me. What do you think his deal is?"*
>
> *"Her mom told me she's divorced, but she told me she's never been married. Obviously, one of them is lying, but why?"*

The list goes on and on and usually in circles.

We hand our imagination over to someone else's plot and forget to write in the pages of our own dreams.

We're killing our stories because you cannot dissect something without killing it!

The most radiant kind of happiness I've witnessed, is in people who aren't concerned with other people's egoic stories about them. They're engaged only in the presence of a story they write from a state of valuing their own worth. Not because they are entitled, but because they understand that they are divine.

They don't allow what other people are writing to bleed through the pages of the novel they are themselves, writing. They appear to have some super shield around them that protects them from the projections of others, or from fear, but

I've found that the super shield is merely a reflection of their willingness to drop their story, to gain themselves. They are empaths to the maximum with serious fucking boundaries who appreciate their own edges in a delicate way. They're the game changers because they know they are not the pawn, but the queen who's finally ready to reign the only territory she's got. Her life.

They are present to what is and happy with what they've written because they know they can always rewrite the next chapter.

They've decided they've seen enough people rewrite history over and over again, so they stopped being one of them. They seek to create a future, outside of the past, which starts with right now.

If someone hands us a pencil and paper to narrate our own lives, we often hand the pencil and paper back, confused by all of the other books we're busy reading, as to what to even say—and we forfeit our moment to write. We're infiltrated by stories we don't even know we're reading by the *he said she said bull shit*, the media, the culture, propagating its historic nonsense. We're too cloudy to write with soul.

At best, we find a way to write with reason.

We're often looking for our answers in someone else's story.

The only place we'll find our happiness is by writing in the pages of our own.

Years back, I was incredibly nervous to meet a man I really wanted. On our first meeting, the entire hour drive to get to him, I sang in my head *(for vibrational effect)* over and over again, "I am beautiful. I love me. I'm excited to meet him and he's excited to meet me."

Of course, I was lying to myself at the time. *(Anyone who has to say that repeatedly for an hour, attempting to create new neuro-pathways of healthy thought patterns is someone who has thought a whole bunch of bullshit, for much too long).*

Regardless, even though I was lying to myself, it was my first attempt at writing a new character positively into my own story.

I was creating the story that *I* wanted rather than playing detective of *his* desires, in hope I might *become* them. He ended up loving me, thinking I was beautiful, and we had a cosmic run of love together that required no detective work. Our relationship inspired only presence.

I may not have believed what I was writing in the sky of my imagination during the car ride to him, but he read it loud and clear.

When thoughts of self-doubt or my hunger for sabotage crept in, I wrote new words. Words I'd never considered writing in the past.

I didn't read into whether what I was writing was true or what he wanted me to write. I wrote what I wanted to have and feel, leaving out the rest.

Writing the story of our own lives commands presence. Presence to what is *true* for us at the soul. It demands our honest focus and never relents. It doesn't dissect motives by walking down the avenues of our incompleteness, but teaches us to accept ourselves, frolicking down the path of our already-present fulfillment.

Playing the detectives in the mysteries of other authors, confuses and distracts us from what's really alive for us. Presence isn't concerned with what *he* said or *she* said if he or she aren't written into our story and saying it, *now*.

Presence is the only place any healing has ever happened in the past, or will ever happen in the future. It's only concerned with experiencing itself *as it is* without making up a motive about someone else's chapter.

It wants to know *itself* through you and for you to know yourself *through* it. Presence has a sensual experience with the awareness of itself, that come out in the form of goosebumps and it wants to be a memory, remembered well.

Presence only hears, feels, tastes and touches itself and it's the heart of true healing.

The moment we give into someone else's drama or begin writing our story in *response* to stories of others, we are merely procrastinating on our own longing to write.

Presence doesn't give a shit if *he* wants you or *she's* lying.

It wants to hold your hand and show you the world right in front of you. The world you've been missing by suffocating your creative potential to come authentically alive by reading summaries of the worlds of others. It wants you to forget everything you've written and everything you've read, so you can *actually*, know *yourself*. It wants to give you juicy sentences that need to be written by your soul and dance with you when you read them back to yourself. It wants you to be quiet and hear them.

Presence wants to be united with you, but it takes practice on your part to unite *with her*.

The instant we dissect something outside of this moment, we're killing the possibility to connect with the peace of what's actually true about our story. If you're reading this, the first miracle is that you are safe, and till death do you part with yourself, you're living with the potential to heal.

Presence longs to have you see yourself in it.

The most radiant happiness I've seen, is from people who create moments they want to be in, rather than distracting themselves with ones *they don't*. They've given up the one thing that holds most of us back: resistance. They gave up the resistance they had, toward the responsibility to show up and be seen as an author. Even if their book is about living alone with a garden never to be read by another soul, they can say it was a life of their own design. They don't need to know how their story is going to end to pick up the pen, they only know they need to write. When they began authoring, happiness met them half way.

They only write stories that feel *right* to them, even if they don't feel *good* to their culture. By way of being present only to the story they are writing, they find a way to live into it. They trust the next page because they know that whatever it is, will feel just as good as now or better. They know this, because they do not have idle hands with their ink. They choose to author.

Their story is written into their radiance and the universe beckons their magic because it recognizes that their radiance simultaneously *commands and experiences* presence.

Secretly, we all want to possess this kind of magic.

We can have it, by writing a story we actually want to be in, a story we wouldn't dare kill. We can have it when we stop weaving our words through the pages of other people's entries.

We're always creating whether we're choosing information to create with that has seeped into our psyches by reading from other authors, or by writing ourselves.

We're even creating stories about other people's stories, just so we don't have to create the one that's screaming inside of us, to write.

May you create a story that comes to know itself fully. A story that only reads by being present to what it, itself, has written, word for word, vision for vision, note for note. A story you no longer dissect to make sense of yourself in.

A story in which you experience each sentence with substance by reading only what is written in the moment and diving into it fully. This is the only way to free ourselves up into knowing what to write next.

A story that's so damn juicy you can taste it in your words.

Not the words of others, but the words that give *your* happiness, *your* authenticity, a voice.

These are the stories of the authors that even after death, do not die.

These are the stories of people who leave legacies.

There are no exceptions to who is allowed to write.

The time to create a new narrative is always.

Writing a story that wasn't handed down to us by generations of oppression, is righting our lineages. It's the breaker of the chains we've been held hostage to since birth that seeps into the marrow of our granddaughters by default.

Write for the sake of my mother, who will likely go to her grave, never giving herself permission to meet the little girl in her who still believes in saving innocence for the sake of itself. Write for the sake of every child that put itself to bed far inside the womb of its body because the world is too scary to stay awake for, who lives an entire life, forgetting to wake itself up. Write for the sake of our earthly lineage and your soul.

Write, for God's sake.

You, creating your own story, is planting your feet firmly in *your real world* and there is nothing braver than daring the real world, with a whole lot of truth.

Acknowledgments

My absolute deepest of gratitude for the tribe that made this possible, named and unnamed, seen and unseen, on earth and above, and to those of you yet to come. To my campaign supporters who've helped move this message from the sky to paper: Kathleen Brown, Neil Nowacki, Deanna Schniers, Sean Nycz, Jessica Vooz, Lauren Oakes, Ken Wareham, Casey Clauser, Jessica Johnson, Dori Micio, Jean Jyotika Skeels, Theresa M. Crandall, Jacqui Becker, Mary Evans, Gus Roszko, Holli Marie, Sanda Sue Weller, Tamara Moselle Oswald, Lindsay DelaFuente, Jessica Kolb, Monica Ganter and lastly, Debbie Hoch, for financially backing this project in a big way. And guys, do not underestimate the amount of healing and change it took to see the last name on that list, reach this page.

33801054R00102

Made in the USA
Middletown, DE
18 January 2019